THE FEAR
DOCTOR

Vince Stevenson

'The real voyage of discovery consists not in seeking new landscapes, but in having new eyes.' – Marcel Proust

'You are smarter than your fears.' – Vince Stevenson

To the three special girls in my life; my wife Gláucia,

my daughter Natália and my mum and starring light, Winnie.

To Kate McNeilly, DTM, my editor.

CONTENTS

ACKNOWLEDGMENTS

To all the people who have invested their time in my teachings. I wish them every continuing success. To the authors of every self-development book I have read for sharing their words and wisdom. This book was inspired by Sydney Banks, Joseph V Bailey, David Bohm, Anthony de Mello, Michael Neill and Jamie Smart (and every philosopher and physicist) who unwittingly kicked my bottom, spun me around and pointed me in the right direction.

FOREWORD

Public speaking is one of life's biggest challenges and it's widely accepted as a problem that we all encounter. It's reportedly life's number 1 fear. We're not born with this essential life skill, it's something we must learn and develop over time. That's why the journey isn't easy, and no two journeys are the same. There are lots of twists and turns, obstacles, detours and jams. Your ego and sensibilities will be battered and bruised. You'll get things wrong and more importantly you'll get things right. You might be a perfectionist and fear every minor and inconsequential fault. If it sounds like you, you'll be exhausted from anxiety but I suggest that you'll find this book comforting and illuminating.

Thankfully, there are valuable tools for exploration. If you have a problem and you're not familiar with the tools for its resolution, anxiety is the inevitable outcome. That said, the value remains in the journey itself. As a speaker, the journey and quest for knowledge and experience never ends. The moment never arrives where you feel that you know enough or can even convey it. As a trainer, I acknowledged that years ago but I didn't sit on my laurels, I started working harder on my education and chose to be the best that I could be at any moment. I know enough for my classroom work and I know a lot more too. That comes in handy at a Q&A. I want to be the best that I can be in the now. That will mean more when you reach the session on metacognition – thinking about thinking.

The reported increase in generalised social anxiety leaves us with an epidemic of anxiety and stress, both at home and in the workplace.

This has a huge impact on self-esteem as the internet has catapulted the spoken word to dizzy heights. YouTube enjoys the distinction of hosting millions of speeches and debates. Every company has a video blog or a communication channel with one employee or another sharing a company update on products, services or plans. There's nowhere to escape. You know you're expected to speak whether you're ready or not. So, why not get ready? The definition of anxiety is – a perceived lack of control over outcomes.

As we will discuss, there are many things that we cannot control. Yet, there are many things that we can control too. Good planning, preparation and practice goes a long way to bolster confidence. Some but not all take this point seriously.

However, we are all different. We have different temperaments and personality attributes. We come from different families with access to different resources. We go to different schools, with different teachers, different structures and emphases. We study different subjects to different levels. We have different friends and influences. We watch different media, follow different politics (actively or passively). We have different jobs with different colleagues and managers under different leadership teams. Not to mention different cultures, creeds, class structures. For those of us with partners and children, there are no two parallel family situations – each one is unique to your specific circumstances. To say that life and public speaking are subjective issues is quite straightforward. So, it's no surprise that public speaking success does not have a one-size fits all solution.

My aim in this book is to move this complex conversation forward. Public speaking is both a psychological and physiological exercise. The best speakers are the ones that aim to master these two complex entities. There's no shortage of good public speakers – though they are not always available when you need them. The great news is that everybody can improve with more knowledge, experience and practice. The key is winning the inner battle. Taming that voice in your head that's trying to hold you back isn't easy, but it is achievable. It doesn't want you to fail. You need to see both triumph and disaster as two imposters (Kipling). A few subtle mindset changes and a greater understanding of belief systems can change your slow, lonely development path for a highway to success.

Each person's life experience triggers numerous problems surrounding public speaking. This book offers numerous insights that with time and practice will form positive solutions.

I mentioned that the journey of the speaker isn't an easy one. And yet, along that path, there is happiness and joy, despair and doubt. It's no different than from the rest of life's investments. What you sow you reap. Life isn't for the faint-hearted and nor is public speaking. Courage is at the heart of this conversation. Courage underpins your journey every step of the way. It begins now with this single step…

Vince Stevenson, 2020

PREFACE

I AM A RECOVERING SPEAKER

In the mid-1980s I had supreme confidence. By the age of 19, I owned a five bedroomed house in Manchester, a relatively flashy car and had undertaken many travels. Add to that a good job, lots of friends and recognition as a footballer and my self-esteem was sky high. By 25, I was a success story. Had I possessed good looks I would have been insufferable. Work was great and life was easy. I was quite the extrovert, almost flamboyant. But how the mighty fall!

I grew up in a time when children were seen and not heard. Opinions were neither sought nor proffered and if I couldn't improve on the silence, I knew to shut up! No complaints. That was the regime of my birth. Sadly, this lack of spoken opportunity did not prepare me for my baptism into the world of professional speaking.

In 1985, after many successful years of low-profile working activity, things took a turn for the worse. My world changed with the arrival of a brown paper envelope. Why was the secretary of the Board of the Co-operative Wholesale Society writing to me? The envelope remained in the tray for almost a week. Every day I picked it up, shook it, sniffed it and checked its weight. There was something suspicious about its energy. Its lurking presence like a black cloud hung over my desk - a horrible distraction. Its contents could only mean one thing - bad news. After a few weeks, I tore it open and confirmed my worst suspicion. I discovered an invitation to speak to the Board in three weeks' time.

I was right. Why me? Why were they picking on me? It was so unfair. I was off the radar. My magnolia personality allowed me to go unnoticed this far and I did not want to speak to them. I could not speak to them. This was the beginning of the end of my naivety.

A harrowing experience ensued. My planning involved staring at a blank piece of paper for days on end. Prayer for the talk's cancellation remained unanswered. Anxiety welled in my chest. I felt dizzy. The shallow character behind the confident smile was on the brink of catastrophe.

When the big day came, I was utterly confused. I tried to make an impression with my clothes. I wore a light blue suit like Don Johnson in Miami Vice, sleeves rolled up to the elbow. This was the fashion of the day although my red plastic shoes were not. Next door to the Boardroom was a bathroom. While washing my hands I made the mistake of opening the faucet too wide and a gush of pressurised water shot into the air. As I recoiled, it splashed over my light blue trousers. It looked like I had peed myself. What a mess! I stood under the hand drier with my pelvis thrust towards the wall as the drier strained to output air. At that moment, middle-aged men in expensive suits entered. They paid a lot of attention to my unnatural stance. It looked like I was trying to limbo into a brick wall.

"You must be Vince," said one of the suits. "Having a bit of trouble?"

"Yes, but it's not what you're thinking," I retorted, "I was just washing my hands when…"

"Come along now, you're on next," he said. "Did you have trouble with the tap?"

"Yes, how did you know?"

"You wouldn't be the first person to come into the Boardroom looking like they'd wet themselves."

I think I should have laughed but how could I? I looked like I had wet myself. As I stepped into the Boardroom, all I could think of was my water stained trousers. First impressions…

After a brief cough, I tried to introduce myself. I cleared my throat and started again. From the outset I saw ten middle-aged faces around the long table. They were in good humour and the energy in the room was high. Perhaps one of them had alerted the others to my trouser predicament.

As I struggled to stand up straight, the room went out of focus. It began to spin to the right before stopping and spinning to the left. The sun streaming in through the window was blinding. I feigned to cough, hoping to buy a moment's pause but that too seemed like a mammoth task of coordination. I think I knew what I wanted to say but my lower jaw felt heavy and I was unable to close my mouth. The motors in my lips failed to shape the syllables of the words and evaporated into nothingness.

My heart lurched and my stomach churned. I lost control of my breathing and I felt my torso collapsing from the outside in. I touched my brow and then dabbed it. I was sweating profusely. One of the suits brought me a folding chair and sat me down. Then he released my tie and collar and another began to fan me with a brown paper folder. After a few moments, I came around from a short tour of oblivion. I could breathe. The mist lifted slightly and there was a glass of water and an electric fan beside me. My eyes perceived life in its usual form. I feigned to stand up and resume my speech but rather like a boxer who had missed the count. Once back on my feet I was ushered out of the room where the receptionist was stirred from her chair to help me. I sat down and held back the tears of innocence. On leaving some while later, everything looked the same as before but with the realisation that the world had turned.

Out of body experiences are overrated. I felt completely crushed - like a juggernaut had squashed my soul. My performance was a complete capitulation and I sensed an intense pain building which led to nausea and more sweating. But that thought soon passed because I knew that I had reserves to combat any situation. I had courage, spirit and resilience on my side. I felt inspired by the entire episode. I recognised that it was not my best moment and neither was it an accurate reflection of my human potential.

The major issue was that my ability to remain invisible as a protection mechanism had failed. Another issue to resolve was that of doing the least possible work while retaining a salaried position. I needed a rethink and a huge upheaval in strategy to move forward. Bravado and irksome egotistical traits are valued in some circles but not it seemed at the Co-op. People prefer substance over show. Was this a spiritual awakening? I hoped so.

This miserable episode began a relentless journey, one which took me around the world, working in a field that I have grown to love. Thirty-five years later, I am still in love with public speaking.

'Whenever we proceed from the known into the unknown, we may hope to understand, but we may have to learn at the same time a new meaning of the word "understanding".' – Werner Heisenberg

Public speaking is a psychological and physiological experience.

There is no shortage of books written on style and delivery. But what happens when you lose control and you can't breathe? People can only achieve delivery mastery when they have conquered their inner conflict, when they have smashed through the anxiety glass ceiling. This book is about winning the inner conflict, and the first lesson is to accept yourself. Next, we build confidence and only then can you explore the voice and develop the rhythm and fluency that will positively impact your audience.

Public speaking is a massive subjective jigsaw. People generally see the pieces but they cannot integrate them into a working whole. There is a lack of clarity around the big picture. Everything in public speaking is a technique. Though nothing in public speaking should ever look like a technique. When driving a car, your visual faculties must align with your hands and feet movements in a seamless fluency. You don't want to grind the gears of your car as you would not allow your voice, words and body language to lack cohesion.

Do you remember your first driving lesson? It wasn't what you expected, was it? Driving is dangerous. It's a huge responsibility to drive a car for fairly clear reasons. You need to read and understand The Highway Code. It's a tricky process, one that we learn to stick with. To achieve mastery in any field you need to ground yourself in the subject's principles and then apply the required techniques when appropriate. The skill is applying the right technique at the right time. For most people, public speaking is not life or death (whatever you tell yourself). As we'll see, whatever you tell yourself will have a profound impact on your outcomes. It's best to ensure that your internal dialogue is of a positive nature and that you show patience with yourself when the going gets tough (as it will from time to time).

Observe great athletes, musicians and stage performers, they make the impossible look common place. It doesn't just happen. It's the result of dedicated focused practice. Look at your life, your profession, your partner and your children. Look at the years of investment in those key relationships. Everything that you value in life takes time to develop and that time was well invested.

So why do we fall short with public speaking? We know that it's not going to kill us, even though driving a car might. The big issue is that of criticism, judgement or public humiliation. We study and work hard and we are told to take life seriously and now our place in our social or professional hierarchy is on the line. That's not actually true, but the way we sell it to ourselves is convincing. As we'll see, we can convince ourselves of anything. We feel that we cannot control the outcomes. This spawns anxiety and then the acute physiological reactions emerge (more on this to come).

Let's look at some typical scenarios where anxiety occurs:

a) asking somebody on a date (rejection hurts)
b) going on that date (will they like me as much as I like them?)
c) exams (have I studied enough? Not studied enough? What are the consequences of failing? Time lost – tuition and exam fees? Resits? Peer pressure? Parental pressure? Humiliation? Damaged self-esteem?)
d) job interviews (Desire to progress and earn a living commensurate with your abilities, providing a home, food a decent life for your family)
e) public speaking (a perceived threat of public humiliation - getting it wrong, letting yourself, team, company, industry down)
f) sporting, musical or performance based public endeavours (can you deliver the goods?)

Anxiety exists when we perceive that we cannot control the outcomes. Anxiety breeds anxiety. The more we think about it, the worse it becomes. Most people suffering anxiety do not understand where the anxiety is coming from and they mistakenly think there is something wrong with them and they experience guilt and a sense of incompleteness. If you're a human being, anxiety is situation normal.

You're alive! You're not ill and you don't need fixing. Isn't that great?

In many things we can't control the outcomes. There are no guarantees in life. I recently pitched a £150,000 project for a charity. I spent two weeks studying the brief and attended three practice sessions. It was exciting entering the Boardroom that day and I recognised the importance of the project for my charity colleagues. So, when my opening statement struck home, I managed to get straight into my flow. I was flying. I had planned in detail, studied the brief and nailed the entire presentation. Everything went according to plan. My charity colleagues expressed their delight. They took me for drinks and dinner, confident that success was ours. Three weeks later we received notice that the funding was allocated to another charity. Massive disappointment!

It's the same with job interviews. You can answer the interviewers' questions brilliantly. You can create a great rapport with them. Your detailed research of their company and their competitors was phenomenal. You really understand the job's detailed requirements. Alas, in life there are no guarantees of anything.

Why do we get anxious? It's because we care about the outcome. You're a human being. It's how you're wired. But all the things we value in life come with a massive investment in our time and energy. If you're not competitive or you don't want a positive outcome enough, you'll be handing your golden opportunities to others. We must prepare ourselves for the competitive rigours of the world.

Just like presentation and job interviews all you can ever do is give it your 100% in the planning, preparation and practice stages. After the session when all is done, detach yourself from the outcome, because it's out of your hands. If there's anything to improve upon then you have something to work on in future. There are always lessons to learn and there is always a next time. You have to be in it, to win it.

'Patience is necessary, and one cannot reap immediately where one has sown.' – Søren Kierkegaard

Public speaking is one of the highest ranked business skills. How you impact people is critical to your success as a human being. It's imperative that you invest time in yourself and above all stay patient. But let me add that you do not need thousands of hours of practice. You can become an effective speaker in one day. I know because I've worked with thousands of students over the years and with correct instruction, students achieve fantastic outcomes. As human beings we love certainty and strive for pleasure. At the opposite end of the spectrum is fear and pain. We do our best to avoid these situations for good reason, because we don't always have the tools or resources to manage them. The basic tools, resources and mindset can be learnt in a day. The rest is to practice rolling it out consistently. Only practice what works for you. Anything else is pointless.

Life is incredibly subjective, as is public speaking. There is no one template for achieving success. It's an exploration of you and your personal attributes. It's an exploration of your knowledge, experience and professionalism. It's an exploration – a fun journey and an incredibly fulfilling experience. Apply these principles from the first opportunity and notice the reduction in anxiety. Your connection with friends, colleagues and family improves. It isn't so much what you say, it's how you make people feel when you say it. Make them feel good, empower them, make them feel capable and you have succeeded in the complex ritual of human connection. Human connection is the whole point of living and leading a meaningful life.

This book's primary aim is to close the gap between how life works and how we believe life works and then apply that to the field of public speaking.

It is a tall order but when we close that gap the world is a better place. There is less anxiety and when you avoid the 'thinking traps', you see that speaking is a golden opportunity. Influencing people in an ethical way is the best job I know. It is not the poison chalice we all too often imagine.

INTRODUCTION

'Courage is knowing what not to fear.' – Plato

The focus of this book is to introduce the principles and discussions explored in my regular workshops. My desire is to help you relinquish negative thought patterns and awaken you. There is autobiographical material that chronicles my changing views, values and experiences. It discusses why I am passionate about public speaking. It alludes to many quotations from physicists, philosophers and spiritual leaders. Its synthesis brings me to this point in my career where I have a valuable story to tell.

If public speaking has ever made you feel foolish or inadequate, you're not alone. Every story, anecdote, metaphor, case study and quotation illustrates a familiar situation. Seeing things in a different light guides you to the truth and beauty of your real self. It's essential to realise that you were born with everything you need to succeed.

'The deepest principle in human nature is the craving to be appreciated.' – William James

PERSONAL

When I was a young man, I was a committed footballer and for many years I played at a semi-professional level. From being a child, football ruled my life. My dedication was obsessive. We didn't talk about OCD in those days, but my passion was all-consuming. Even cleaning my muddy boots immediately after arriving home in preparation for next week's game was part of the ritual. It was best not to stand in my way when talking matters football. I was crazy about training. I didn't drink or smoke and I managed a healthy diet. I went to bed early. I spent spare time visualising scoring goals or making vital interceptions. I took yoga lessons to relax and recover between matches. I played in many tours to Europe and I learned so much from the privilege of travel. It broadened my horizons and it took me to the most fabulous countries.

The whole issue of obsessive thinking and behaviour fuelled my desire to play at the highest level. Playing football, just like booking your summer holiday fills you with hope and adrenaline. Football was a pleasure and a devotion which filled my life with purpose. It was my escape. Perhaps when other things let me down, I always knew that football would be there for me. It was the most enjoyable aspect of my life. More than anything it gave me a sense of connection. People appreciated me. I felt valued by significant others (my family, teachers and community). People in the game knew me and they kept in touch. Managers called, asking if I would consider playing for their teams. This did wonders for my self-esteem and all I had to do was play a game I loved.

'A coward dies a thousand deaths, a brave man but once...' – *Julius Caesar* - Shakespeare

Football is wonderful when you're winning and yet all the good things happened to me after I learnt to lose. At secondary school, I was a goalkeeper, a good goalkeeper but not a busy goalkeeper. Not busy, because the team in front of me always won, they kept me well protected and I rarely got my shorts dirty. Then in the 3rd year, a new school opened nearby and they too had a reputation for winning. As our first fixture loomed, I became more and more anxious about losing. So much so, I told my sports master that I was injured and that I was unable to play. This created a big problem for him because there was no official reserve keeper. Eventually, my friend Gary was cajoled into playing. I suddenly felt guilty that this poor chap was standing in for me when I wasn't injured and that the inevitable defeat could be blamed on his lack of experience or ability.

Something both wonderful and tragic happened that day. We won 1-0 and Gary made a succession of excellent saves. He was proclaimed man of the match and he replaced me in goal for the next six months. Throughout the game as he was pulling off these incredible saves, I kept saying to myself, 'that should be me'. I realised that I had given up my position of 'power' in a silly attempt to protect my egoistical pride. What if we had lost 1-0 or 5-0 or any other score? Big deal! Playing the game is the game. You can't show how good you are from the side lines. You need to be out there in the thick of it. Win or lose. You can't choose your games. Your games choose you. Had Gary not moved to another part of the country, I may never have got my place back and I might have lost all interest in football. I'm glad I didn't, but it was a hard and painful lesson. It has given me the rest of my life to reflect on that ludicrous decision. While Gary was keeping my place warm, the District team was selected and I wasn't in it because I was side lined. The matches were watched by talent scouts from the best clubs in the north-west. I missed my chance of being spotted and perhaps becoming a professional footballer. I only had myself to blame.

> 'You are all enlightened beings. You are all Buddhas pretending not to be. It is my duty to expose you.' – Bhagwan Shree Rajneesh - Osho

I have a healthy interest in physics and philosophy. They called early scientists 'natural philosophers.' Scientists and philosophers search for the truth. On my journey as a speaker I have researched the anatomy and physiology of the body; the respiratory system, the central nervous system, neuroscience and everything down to cellular level. I have studied psychology and particularly the psychology of public speaking. Let me ask you a question. Two twins have the same physical attributes and lived under the same roof for 21 years. One of them is a brilliant speaker and works for an NGO. The other lacks confidence and belief and attends my fear of public speaking class in London. Why is the playing field not even?

My desire is to pull the strands of public speaking together in a subjective contextual framework. This framework embraces the development process for speaking. It recognises the business world's desire that we change at its phenomenal pace. We need to develop our technical and personal skills in the race for resources. If you're not moving forwards, then you're sliding backwards. Change is good, especially when we choose how and when to change. When change is an imposition it creates anxiety. That's something we should avoid in all its disguises.

My most profound belief is that anybody who wants to be an effective speaker quickly becomes one. Everybody has what it takes because they were born with everything they need to succeed. There is a seed of greatness within you right now. Objectivity around your capabilities is not easy. You are too close, so you focus on the negative aspects of your nature. We are drawn to catastrophe like moths to a light. You can't see what I can see and it's my job to highlight and draw out your inner potential. It is my duty to expose your latent capabilities and help you become the person, the speaker and the leader that you want to be.

Before we move into main issues, let me ask you a few questions. If you're stuck in your thinking and not making progress, we need to start being open to the possibility of effective change.

What would becoming a good speaker mean to you and what will it do for you on a day to day basis? How would your life change? How would you react to that change?

When will you know that you're a good speaker?

Would you be open to the possibility that the change starts right now?

PART 1

WHAT'S GOING ON

UPSTAIRS?

PSYCHOLOGY

Metacognition, Heuristics, Pain, Beliefs, Compartmentalisation

'The brain can remember, feel, believe, calculate, extrapolate, infer and deduce. It does everything that we think of as thinking.' – Professor Steven Novella

Student: You can understand why people thought the sun went around the earth.

Ludwig Wittgenstein: Why would you say that?

Student: Because it looks that way.

Ludwig Wittgenstein: And how would it look if it didn't?

This section is about thinking about thinking, or metacognition. In the following sections, I will discuss thinking patterns that we either acknowledge or ignore. If you spend little time thinking about your thinking, you will find this section particularly valuable. When you recognise how your mind works you start making modifications in your approach to thinking which benefits outcomes. Critical thinking skills are valued as they help you understand how you perceive the world. You can then identify how others perceive the world while sharing the same circumstances. Challenging misconceptions is a useful investment in time. Everything that brings greater experiential clarity to your world is of the highest value.

The human brain is an evolutionary triumph. It is the most complex entity in the known universe. Since the dawn of primitive life forms, the developing brain has questioned the puzzle of its surroundings. Our 21st-century brain is a hybrid of our various stages of progress. It includes the reptilian, mammalian, primate and now the human brain with the impressive frontal lobes of the neocortex. This functionality provides mankind with the learning capacity, vision and critical thinking skills to understand its world and venture beyond into others.

Man's potential is as astonishing as it is limitless. Through determination and collaborative scientific work, our ability to harness and manipulate nature creates in many, great hope for the future. Yet in others, man's power resting in the hands of the powerful few is a bubbling cauldron of concern. We manipulate the atom to generate energy for homes, schools and hospitals. We create nuclear weapons with similar technology.

Though the wonders of the human brain are remarkable and infinite it remains a flawed organ. It is easily deceived and it follows that its decisions and conclusions are often inaccurate. The first deceptive illusion is that we look out through our eyes and observe the world. This is a basic misunderstanding. As light streams in through the iris, the optic nerve which is part of the central nervous system transmits visual information to the brain. The brain asks the question, what must be out there to create this representation? At that point, it constructs our perception and experience of life moment to moment. Where information is missing it fills in the blanks. The work of Hermann von Helmholtz in the 19th-century was critical to the beginning of this understanding.

Perception is construction. It's a continuous process, every waking moment and even while we're asleep, the brain perceives and constructs. Have you ever had a dream or a nightmare? The brain perceives and constructs while we sleep. Some find that scary. It's happening outside of your control and as humans we love to exercise control. In shared circumstances like attending sporting events or perhaps a church service, everybody perceives and constructs that experience independently and uniquely. Through this simple fact alone, there are seven billion different interpretations of perception and reality at any one moment. More than enough ammunition for the endless conflict that arises in the world. Life becomes harder when we can't reconcile differences within ourselves.

We are primarily social animals. We enjoy the love of close family and we seek acceptance from broader society. It's an unpleasant experience if teased as an adolescent about our hair, clothes or friends. We have an ego (self-image) which grows and develops as we mature. Our self-esteem is an invaluable facet of personality. We begin to take life seriously and assume our place in society. We appreciate others who respect our contribution. We have a public face and nobody likes to lose face. That calling for high esteem remains with us throughout life. We stand up and speak up for ourselves. Our desire for natural justice helps us follow through with our aspirations. If we do not, nobody will know who we are or what we stand for, or take us seriously.

Humans are emotional beings. We experience hunger, fear, lust, regret, love, disappointment and elation. We make decisions based on what we think makes us feel good or indeed are right for us. Only after we have made the decision do we consider rationalising it. As we get older, we don't make better decisions we become better at rationalising them. Examine your thoughts, beliefs and actions and ask which comes first, emotion or logic?

I recently bought a £300 home study course from a university in California. My living room contains books and educational resources cluttering the floor and shelves. In view of several thousand pounds worth of resources that I haven't managed to study yet, was it a logical or an emotional decision? It was an emotional decision. I bought what I wanted. It pleased me to buy it. Owning these materials makes me feel strong and I believe that I'm moving forwards in my life and career. Spending on personal development is an investment. I'm a quick learner. It's good to have options. I also remember the days when I invested nothing in my personal development. The dire consequences of my poor investment awaits in later sections.

My wife's perspective is that our income is better spent on saving for a larger house or sending our daughter to a private school. It would be impossible for me to achieve any of the major items on that wish list for £300 which is my logical obstacle. So, I invoke a confirmation bias. This is where I cherry-pick information that backs up my decision. I ignore, distort or delete information that contradicts it. My wife's point that I should first study the materials cluttering the living room is a valid point. A valid point that I choose to ignore.

When you go for a job interview, what human attributes do you choose to display? We talk about academic background, work experience and achievements. There is no discussion about emotional traits. Do you want to show your emotional exuberance or bitter disappointments at the interview? We are emotional beings and we prefer to display the logical side of our capability and potential. Research demonstrates that interview panels select candidates from emotional rationale. What transcends academic background, work experience and achievement is whether the panel like you. If they feel the chemistry between you, them and the company is a good fit for the future, you're in.

Our human experience requires that we utilise mind and memory. If we didn't, we'd have to relearn every valuable life lesson several times per day which is inefficient and would contribute to our early demise as living creatures. Memory is a major factor and many people report that their memories are poor. They scold themselves for not remembering significant dates, like wedding anniversaries and clients' names. Students attend classes at school or university and can't remember anything important forty-five minutes later. When pressed, they'll pluck out a few headings and then scrape together some facts or examples. Their minds distort, delete and elaborate scant information and arrive at inexact or valueless conclusions.

'It is the mark of an educated mind to be able to entertain a thought without accepting it.' – Aristotle

Look at how optical illusions play with the brain. Through ambiguous illusions, distortions, paradox illusions and fictions, the brain is tricked into perceiving something other than what is. Artists create three-dimensional perspective on a two-dimensional canvas. Static objects and lines appear to flash or move. Objects and scenes that look like one thing become something else.

Magicians have long exploited the limitations of our brain. They perform simple close-up tricks or create spectacular illusions. Their magic looks real and credible and yet it's a brain distortion. A trick of the mind, usually involves some form of misdirection. Misdirection diverts the eye and attention away from the key action. The eyes and the brain have a tough job managing our perception moment to moment. The brain asks the question, what must be out there to create this?

Delusion is another trick of the mind where we hold a false belief against all evidence. In 2008, the media reported that a red panda had escaped from Amsterdam zoo. There were over 600 reported sightings in the next few days. The panda's body was found in the confines of the zoo and an autopsy indicated that the creature had died before it was reported missing. Six hundred reported sightings!

In Manchester, many years ago, my girlfriend had short black hair and wore a distinctive blue raincoat. After a few years, the relationship ended. Because I missed her, I saw her many times in shops, on the bus or walking down the street. On each occasion, upon closer inspection, it was another woman with a similar raincoat/hairstyle.

How can that be? It's simple. We see what we want to see. We take fragments of information and then construct a 'memory'. It does not have to be real to look real. The brain perceives and constructs.

In 1995, I was working in Hinckley in Leicestershire. Reports of unidentified flying objects started to headline in the local newspaper. Nothing unusual there. Reports of UFOs first materialised in the late 1970s. I observe that there were sightings up to 2010. Bright and credible colleagues reported they had seen UFOs. Yet, there is no hard evidence of UFO activity, although it featured as the interesting topic of conversation at work for some considerable time.

The ability to speculate and exaggerate is part of human experience. Without speculation and deduction, there could be no scientific progress. Scientific scepticism is necessary to ensure that we have a firm basis for establishing the truth (as far as possible). It's also part of the human condition to search for the truth, unless you have a vested interest in concealing it, of course. Murderers try and cover their tracks and bank robbers hide their identities. Governments and large corporations conceal bad economic data that affects confidence and rocks stock market values. Car manufacturers lie about emissions testing. Some banks have rigged interest rates and handled money and accounts used in terrorism and money laundering. Whatever the event, people tend to act and react in a way from which they will derive the greatest benefit. People are driven by self-interest.

On the lighter side, as my daughter has grown up, it's become a regular event to watch The X Factor. The first few weeks of auditions are wonderful. We see talented people across a broad spectrum of disciplines and/or musical genres and we have also witnessed the deluded who fall into two categories: the seriously deluded who believe they have the talents required to bring international fame. Secondly, those with no talent, who know they have no talent and are happy to mock themselves in front of the panel, a live audience of thousands and a TV audience of millions.

The abuse and derision have no impact on this latter group. Indeed, it seems to make them stronger and more resilient to the panel's comments and negative public reaction. The deluded have no control over what the panel and audience have in store for them. Their delusion helps them rationalise that the panel's decision and the audience's reaction is flawed. In time both the panel and the audience will see the error of their ways. Contestants often return in different costumes in later years to repeat the process. Why do 'rational' beings put themselves through it? It runs contrary to the primary human desire of having control and preserving high self-esteem.

If you are somewhat talented and not yet star material, your ego feels that it's under attack. It looks like the world is conspiring against you and your circumstances are provoking emotions better subdued. These contestants go away, rehearse and return better, stronger and more resilient in future series. I have the greatest admiration for this category. They possess courage, talent and indefatigability.

Strange as it may seem, people believe in the Loch Ness monster, the Yeti and North America's 'Bigfoot' (a US type Yeti (but not snowy)). Can you advance any credible evidence to support their existence? Flaky black and white footage from 50 years ago doesn't count. Nor do images of giant footsteps in the snow. As a child, I loved these stories. Isn't it great to think that there's more to life than can be explained? Although I never believed in them, I enjoyed their curiosity value. Imagination is greater than knowledge – to an extent.

Like the UFO issue, sensible people offer their 'evidence' and stand by their 'sightings'. There is special pleading that because we cannot explain something, it does not mean that it could not be real if we maintain an open mind. Arguments of special pleading for Bigfoot and the Yeti are tragic. Because we have yet to capture these creatures, who is to say that they do not have supernatural powers like making themselves invisible? Again, it's a lovely story, but as there is no evidence of other species on this planet with magical powers. I conclude that it's a gigantic nonsense although I am happy to be wrong.

Crop circles fooled and divided expert opinion for decades. I thought it was fascinating and mysterious although we now know it was a massive hoax. Even the logical mind and creator of Sherlock Holmes, Sir Arthur Conan Doyle was fooled by the story of the Cottingley Fairies. In the later stages of his career, Conan Doyle had stopped writing fiction as his new passion was advancing the cause of spiritualism. Although he received a large fee for the article and pictures, he made the decision because the pictures furthered his personal aims. Soon after, he found them to be nothing more than a childish hoax. This is just one example that proves that sensible, intelligent, rational people believe what they want to believe. It doesn't need to be true.

Conspiracy theories exist in most aspects of life, you need only listen to office gossip. Here are some examples drawn from politics, sport and business.

The JF Kennedy conspiracy is the most famous of the 20th-century. The theory goes that it would be impossible for one man to plan, resource and finally execute the President from a roof top in Dallas. Why wasn't the President better protected? He must have needed the help and collaboration of a body like the CIA. It was an inside job… Fifty years later despite heavy scrutiny, there is still no credible evidence that Lee Harvey Oswald had accomplices.

In the 1998 World Cup Final, hosts France played tournament favourites Brazil. The night before the match, Brazil's talisman striker Ronaldo suffered a seizure and the following day it was announced that he was unfit to play. As one of the world's leading stars, the timing of the event was a sporting tragedy. Yet minutes before kick-off the news filtered through that Ronaldo would play after all. Although he was present on the pitch, his contribution suggested that he was ill.

France won 3-0 and the whole match and spectacle was an anti-climax. There is still something of a mystery surrounding the circumstances leading up to kick-off. One theory was that Brazil's players received millions of dollars to allow the hosts to win. Some said that Brazil would host a future World Cup Finals for losing that one game. Many years later, there is still no evidence of any 'foul play'. If you were to ask a millionaire World Cup finalist about the choice of corrupt money or becoming a footballing legend, which do you think he would take?

If it were true, by now somebody would have sold their story. It would be difficult to keep a lid on such a momentous event with so many people involved. This story isn't plausible.

Finally, I read a great deal that the development of electric cars and clean energy processes are scuppered by the gas-guzzling oil industry which fears that it will lose its energy market monopoly. Their strategy is to poison ideas, buy up patents, kill projects with bad press, harass individuals and buy alternative energy companies in their infancy to prevent them coming to fruition. As always, there's lots of talk and no evidence. Tesla cars seem to make a nonsense of that claim.

Why do people love conspiracy stories? Conspiracy stories confirm the notion that the establishment is out to get us, fool us or manipulate us. We harbour the thought that the 'establishment' calls the shots. It looks like others decide our success and failure. For some, abdicating responsibility for their outcomes is quite a relief. For others it's the signal to dig in deeper and try even harder. As mentioned, the majority of us love the thought of having control over our lives.

At the end of the day, what you think and feel matters. If you believe something, it will shape your behaviours and the parameters of your world. Truth and beliefs are not always the same thing. For centuries, man believed the earth was flat. Is it flat? The Aztecs sacrificed their children on their pyramids to thank the Gods for a good harvest. Would they do that now? I'm sure there's a law against it. When you were a child, did you believe in Father Christmas? Did that shape a behaviour? Did you look forward to your presents every year? Just because you believe something, doesn't mean that it's true. It just means that you believe it.

Heuristics – 'Nothing in life is as important as you think it is when you are thinking about it.' – Daniel Kahneman

Due to time critical criteria have you ever made a snap decision? Do you make intelligent guesses? Have you ever made a big decision based on intelligent guesswork and later found out that it was wrong? Did that decision cost you money, a job, a friend, a partner? Did you regret making it? Would you make a similar decision again in similar circumstances? That's a lot of questions, to which the answer is, most people do.

Throughout my life, I have made many snap decisions based on insufficient and unreliable evidence. I have regretted many decisions and as time has progressed, I do my best not to fall into this heuristic trap. Heuristics are rules of thumb, pigeon holes, stereotypes, or mental shortcuts that lead to suboptimal decision making.

We make judgments on all types of things; posh accents, rough voices, where people live, their hobbies and interests, their social ambitions or lack of, the way they dress and with whom they associate. We all think we're great at 'reading' people and yet we are not. If you were to document the times you got it wrong you would amass a comprehensive 'dodgy dossier' of bad decisions.

Heuristics are based on thoughts, assumptions, feelings and unreliable evidence. One of the traps is to believe that we're too busy to spend time and resources on making balanced decisions. We need a decision straight away. As your 'to do' list grows and time pressure increases, the more likely we'll opt for a heuristic decision. Except for the medical profession and perhaps civil engineering, few decisions are of life and death significance.

Students tell me that they've purchased cars online without a mechanical inspection. They hire builders without qualifications or testimonials. They bought timeshare property under the influence of the vendor's alcohol. 'The price was great and I went for it', they tell me. When the deal looks too good to be true, it usually is. Salesmen like to confuse us with their bundled offers and self-imposed sales deadlines. I can offer you 30% off that price up to midnight. We are pressured and coerced into decision making for fear of losing the 'bargain'. If we're making this kind of flawed decision with significant sums of money, what about your smaller decisions? Can you trust them?

A recent dilemma I've explored was choosing my daughter's ballet company. There are three ballet companies within a mile of where we live. None of them has a great reputation based on information obtained from the local ballet outfitters shop. This was my only source of 'credible' information – let's call her lady X. On the far side of town there's another ballet group which has large fees and excellent teachers. The downside is that it's a long way and on the wrong side of the infamous one-way system. The ballet lesson lasts 45 minutes which is insufficient time to come home during the class.

My assumptions and bias are that this journey after a hard day's work may prove to be the tipping point with my daughter and her many activities. This option demands that I am home on a Wednesday evening and that the car is available. The prospect of my wife and daughter catching many buses in the dark and braving winter temperatures is too much of a strain on my marriage.

It's hard to believe that three local ballet classes are as awful as suggested. Perhaps lady X is showing some form of bias towards these companies in view of previous difficulties. Time is a big issue for me. Do I have time to visit and assess three local companies and make an informed decision on their comparative offerings? That statement makes the assumption that I have objective criteria on which to base my decision. I know nothing about ballet or ballet teachers.

So, what did I do? I took my daughter to all three companies who kindly allowed her to observe a class. She met the teachers and many of the students and I spoke to parents who were happy with the fees and facilities. I asked where best to buy my daughter's ballet gear and they suggested not at lady X's shop.

My daughter made the final decision when she recognised one of her school friends in class. She had attended one of the companies for years and remained happy there. It was also possible to share the driving duties with her mother. The due diligence exercise was a great success. It was a worthwhile investment in my time and my daughter's development. I want to kick myself for all the bad and lazy decisions that I've made over the years. Now that I'm aware of how I arrived at those bad decisions, I have changed and improved the thinking and decision-making process.

COMPARTMENTALISATION

'The first principle is that you must not fool yourself and you are the easiest person to fool.' – Richard Feynman

After the Co-op debacle my ego suffered. At least that's what I told myself*. That steamroller effect played on my mind for months. My secret was in the hands of the Board. I didn't think it appropriate to discuss with my friends or family. I thought I'd best keep it to myself as I was struggling to reconcile the situation. I noticed that I was able to function with my work, though I felt empty or somehow incomplete. I expected a follow up discussion (which never occurred.*) Or a suggestion either to seek professional help or indeed leave the company (which never occurred.*) So, I carried on expecting one day to walk down the corridor to peals of laughter as my colleagues pointed at the sweaty guy (which never occurred.*) I continued to play and enjoy life as a confident footballer. In football, your performance depends on your physical presence; your fitness and your ability to acquit yourself on the field. Though I struggled with this negative experience, a new belief emerged. It occurred to me that I was much better at speaking than I demonstrated on that day. That was not a true representation of my potential, either as a speaker or as a human being. I knew instinctively that I was better than that, even though there was no evidence yet.

*These were all thoughts. They seemed real and they were not. The mind is deceptive. You can convince yourself of anything.

I noticed that it was easy to compartmentalise my feelings. My speaking disappointment had not interfered in the other aspects of my life where I was stepping forward. What helped the reconciliation process was my experience as a footballer. I knew that if I wanted to progress to a higher level, I had to submit to the sacrifice and disciplines of success. I needed to undertake some intelligent practice.

I wasn't born to become a footballer. It happened because of my unswerving focus on discipline. The better my planning, preparation and practice, the better the results flowed. There was a direct correlation. To become a good speaker, I would have to discover and follow the correct path. So, my first task was to find an outstanding mentor (not easy pre-internet). Make a coherent plan, identify a creditable purpose that was consistent with my abilities and execute the plan. This was easier said than done.

Like football, speaking is a skill. All skills consist of underlying component techniques. By understanding and practising the answers to how and why questions, you become more comfortable with the task in hand. Understanding is the first step. Practise is the second. The Highway Code is an invaluable theoretical resource – but it tells you nothing about the practicalities of driving a car. When how meets why - something phenomenal happens in terms of confidence and delivery. The success criteria for driving a vehicle are clearly defined. The standards are objective. In public speaking, we'll find that it's more subjective.

I am making an enormous assumption that your motivation is high, and you want to become an active speaker. You can only achieve that by regular practice, trial and error, and with the benefit of objective, supportive and constructive feedback.

'The unexamined life is not worth living.' – Socrates

We think all day every day. We live in a psychological reality where we experience life through our thoughts, moment to moment. When we're awake we say we are conscious and yet not always consciously aware of what is going on around us. If it's not in your thinking, to all intents and purposes, it doesn't exist.

Since you started reading this book, 3000 children in Africa have died of malaria and malnutrition. If that horrible statistic is not in your thinking then it doesn't register. If the 4.2 million children living in poverty in the UK are not in your thinking then we have a similar situation. Now that you know about these two issues, what are you going to do about it? Well, you could take action. You could find out more information and volunteer to help or perhaps make a charitable donation. Or you could choose to do nothing. You compartmentalise it and move on to the next paragraph. I am not making any judgments here about your thinking and actions (or mine for that matter). I am just saying that this is the way it works.

I had a lot of problems and inappropriate thoughts swirling around my head when I first began my public speaking career. I told myself that 'I am not good enough. Nobody will listen to me. I'm not the sort of person who can succeed. I have seen good speakers and they make it look so easy. That isn't me. I'm not made that way. Never in a million years was I born to be a good speaker.'

Many years later, I am told I am a 'successful' speaker. By that I mean, I work in class most days and receive good feedback. Every year I receive invitations to speak at events in London, across the UK and throughout the world. In recent years, I delivered training in France, Bangladesh, Romania, Brazil, Malta, the Faroe Islands and Mauritius. This year I have possibilities with Azerbaijan, Nigeria, Switzerland and South Africa, all these international invitations were the direct result of student referrals. I hope I'm on the correct development path.

For the last ten years, I have delivered approximately 50 scheduled training courses per year as well as private 1-2-1 sessions with executives from the broadest spectrum of finance, industry, public and third sector organisations. I have attended a speakers' club meeting every week for the last 15 years. I have also judged many speech contests at club, area, district, national and international levels.

Many years ago, I fell in love with public speaking. Which begs the question, how did I go from trembling wreck to proficient speaker? How was it done?

The first thing you have to do is change your relationship with public speaking. Moving the mindset from negative (anxious/ nervous/ apprehensive) to positive (gratitude/happy/excited) is essential.

Understanding my thoughts and behaviours and the behaviours of others has unlocked my potential to help. When we're anxious we're focused on internal chatter, when we're talking, we need to take that same energy and focus it outward. When a singer or performer takes the stage, they must shut down all cognitive dissonance and focus on delivering great value in that moment. Actors and athletes must calm their doubts and self-limiting thoughts that block stellar performance. Do the right thing for your audience and they'll be with you all the way.

Compartmentalisation is the key and it's something that I first learned as an aspiring footballer and then as an improving speaker/trainer. The concept is simple. When you stand up to do your thing, you park all the outstanding issues in your life and you focus on the activity. A batsman playing cricket needs to play each ball received as it comes. He has to ignore his form (good or bad); his reputation, the bowler's reputation, the team's position in the table, his average, his captain, what his dad said that upset him that morning, what he had for breakfast and whatever, he thinks about politics and the price of fish. You have to play each ball on its merits. Football was my great escape from the world. It took me out of my daily life and delivered me to another world.

'Never mind the ball – get on with the game.' – Dave McCormack

One Monday morning in the late 1980s, I went to work to find the office almost empty and those in attendance were somewhat subdued. I searched through my messages guessing that I had forgotten to attend an important meeting. A few colleagues arrived and we all failed to resolve the empty office puzzle. Half an hour later we received notice of imminent redundancy.

For me, it wasn't a great job. I didn't like my boss - his brand of leadership - and I didn't enjoy the work. I didn't spend too much time worrying about the situation as that could wait until tomorrow. That night I was playing in the FA Cup.

The FA Cup was always a huge buzz for me. Without sounding defeatist, I think we all know that non-league clubs don't reach the FA Cup final. The beauty of competitive sport is to play at the highest level. In football it's one against one and eleven against eleven. Win your individual battle. Anything can happen - you can play above yourself. You can surprise yourself and answer any doubters with your performance. You play for your pride and you play for your team mates.

Considering I had recently moved to London and taken on a £100,000 mortgage at 15% interest, some friends called my approach foolish. But I think I had clarity in my thinking and I focused on the task at hand. The following day came soon enough and I gave the job hunting my full attention. In the late 1980s, redundancy became the norm. There was no stigma attached as in previous years. I found it easy to compartmentalise my thoughts and reconcile them. Though at that point I began to wonder how long it would take to secure a new job.

For me redundancy was a good thing. It ended a poor working relationship that I should have ended myself. Yet, my colleague Bob who was single and about my age, saw redundancy as a betrayal and a personal rejection by the company. His behaviour made him aggressive and erratic. It wasn't redundancy that was creating the problem. It was his thoughts around redundancy which triggered his behavioural issues and resulted in his earlier than scheduled dismissal.

'Fortune favours the prepared mind.' – Louis Pasteur

'My last speech was a disaster. I thought I'd wing it.'

This is a flawed choice and bad decision-making.

'I was so anxious about my last speech I didn't start preparing until the night before. Then I couldn't sleep. The next day I was like a zombie.'

This too is a flawed choice and bad decision-making.

'I delegated the slides to my team. There was a mix up over the dates and I felt really silly at the meeting.'

It's essential we take responsibility for our actions. Delegation is not abdication. It's hard to believe that these scenarios were the product of an intelligent and capable person. It's even harder to imagine that an organ as well developed as the human brain would arrive at such conclusions.

I am still kicking myself now. How could I get it so wrong?

Pain, learning and experience – man and the animal kingdom

A thoroughbred racehorse lives a luxurious life. It has five-star accommodation, food, heating and medical attention. It lives to a strict regime in its yard and as its first race approaches, the pattern of its life changes. The training becomes more intensive. The jockey races it against other horses from the stable. The horse sees the whip as a speed 'motivator'. As the big race approaches it undergoes many experiential changes. When it's transported to the racetrack it meets unfamiliar horses in that yard. There are different stables and surroundings. Then there's the comings and goings of the stable lads as they arrive and prepare for the race followed by cantering down past a grandstand of noisy punters. Then there's the excitement and anxiety of waiting in the racing stalls. It's an alien experience for this beautiful creature. It runs against other novices and it may run well and win or it may not. Whatever the result, it's a trial of training and temperament. It's a new experience and the horse learns much as it grows, develops and matures. So long as it remains strong and healthy it continues to improve its performance. Animals have great memories and they're great learners. Ask any dog owner. We humans are just the same, though we often exclude ourselves from learning opportunities. Many people feel that their education ends with school or university and for some it does. In a fast-changing world, that person is in danger of becoming a dinosaur. If we're not learning, changing and adapting every day, we're sliding into the abyss.

Let's talk about bullfighting for a few moments. Do you know what happens when a bull survives the ring? The rule was that it returned to its breeder. With its job done, it eats grass and continues propagating the species. In Spain in the 1930s, there was a shortage of fighting bulls, so unscrupulous breeders put them forward multiple times. The law was for the protection of the matador. Bulls are dumb, but they are by no means, stupid creatures. When the matador shows the red cape and the bull goes one way, and the matador the other, the bull learns this trick. Bulls are not interested in tradition, spectacle or 'artistry'. Hemingway, in *Death in the Afternoon* once described a rogue breeder who allowed his bull into the ring over twenty times. Imagine that bull in an extreme and hostile environment with picadors pushing mini javelins into its shoulders. All its painful memories enraged. We all have powerful memories around the subject of pain, as do bulls. Twenty visits to the ring suggest A&E for the matador.

On my daughter's third birthday I bought her first bicycle. The sun shone down as I lifted it from the back of the car and rested it against the garden wall. My daughter was ecstatic. We sat on the doorstep, I assembled the stabilisers and pumped up the tyres. When finished, I said, "Natalia, don't touch the bicycle while Daddy goes to the shed. I need to bring the spanner to tighten up the bolts. Promise me not to touch the bike." She nodded.

Two minutes later, I returned, and there she lay on the ground with the bike between her legs; she was screaming. There is quite a slope on the brick forecourt, and her first attempt at solo bike riding resulted in scraped knees and bruised elbows. The sobbing continued for some time. I took her by one hand and lifted the bike with the other and began to lead her to the house - but Natalia was still game. Immediately she stopped screaming and began to wrestle the handlebars from me. The pain of not riding was far greater than the pain of falling off. She composed herself, dusted off her clothes, gave me a determined look and got back on the bicycle. When courage is so strong, it far outweighs the pain.

Both the animal kingdom and man alike have intelligence, strength and depths of resilience. The moment you abandon these attributes the problem becomes intractable.

BELIEFS

Our beliefs show up in all aspects of our lives on a day to day basis. We cherish our beliefs because they are the fabric of who we are. Our beliefs are emotional investments that we grow and nurture throughout time. Sometimes it feels like we are inseparable from our beliefs. They are so deep rooted they have a significant impact on our day to day behaviours. A belief does not have to be true or proven, we just need hold it.

So why do we hang on to our beliefs when new information comes in or better ways of interpreting information arise? Cognitive dissonance arises when mutually exclusive beliefs are not reconciled. We compartmentalise these conflicting beliefs, but as human beings we prefer grand unified solutions. To move forward, we have to recognise that our beliefs are open to revision. How many times in your life have you recognised that something you once believed no longer applies? It hurts at first because we are emotional creatures. We invest in our emotions and then backfill them with the power of distorted logic. We are excellent at rationalising our worst or even most offensive public behaviours. It looks like our circumstances are conspiring to make us behave in this way and in believing that we negate the truth of choice. At every decision point in our day, we have the opportunity of exercising a choice. So, what happens when we're wrong about our beliefs and choices?

Public consistency

We have a desire to remain comfortable with ourselves. We like to be rock solid, dependable individuals. People want to be with us. They know who we are and what we stand for. We enjoy and exude a consistent persona, one that appeals to ourselves and others. Look at the many fallen politicians who say one thing and then do something else. Even after their conviction for criminal offences they often report 'they feel vindicated in their actions. They've had their day in court and the truth is now in the public domain'. They find it unbearable to accept their inconsistencies or admit an error of judgment. For public figures, this is the beginning of the end of their careers. That said we all like to be consistent in our behaviours in public.

We have experienced many changes in the thinking paradigm of the day. *The earth goes around the sun and not the sun around the earth.* That single assertion cost many people their lives. It flew in the face of what was then 'conventional wisdom'.

The sun rises in the east and sets in the west. That isn't true either but they still teach it in school. It looks like the sun rises in the east and sets in the west but that's an illusion; a beautiful illusion and an impressive illusion, but just an illusion. Hundreds of years later, we look back on medieval science and scoff at their errors. Nobody wants to accept that they're wrong. Governments who change course on their policies are accused of U-turns by their opponents. Governments now talk of pragmatic long-term strategy and 'wiggle room' to make tactical changes.

For those of us not in the public spotlight, it's much easier to move forward. Once I recognise and reconcile a belief change, I branch off into the direction that will bring the greatest reward. When the soil in the old field is exhausted, it's best to begin ploughing in a different field. You don't need to announce it, just move on. It's only a big deal if you make it a big deal in your thinking. We have to accept that throughout our lives significant change occurs. Change that occurs of our own volition is the best change. There is no tension because you're aligned to the outcomes of your intention. When change arises from external circumstances, we are less flexible and less disposed to the outcomes. Indeed, we are often resistant because the outcomes can be detrimental to our interests.

Beliefs change. Life goes on. We change. We move on.

In my classroom sessions, the students make many speeches and we review them on video. At the end of day one, we review the last speech and we discuss the success criteria agreed in the morning. Then we apply it to each speech and each speaker. Though the delivery progress is significant, few students choose to accept their improvements. We hear the words, 'It's better than I thought. I'm not as bad as I was. I'm having a good day at last.' To accept the evidence that they're improving contradicts their belief system. Even when it's untrue, students insist on remaining consistent with their previous negative views. I am relentless in exposing the truth. In time they get it. They see and feel the difference. That's why I love my work. The look of relief is phenomenal. It's not unusual too for tears to be shed in class.

'Surrender to what is. Let go of what was. Have faith in what will be.' – Sonia Ricotti

So, what happens when we are wrong? All beliefs are subject to change and revision.

As a child I grew up in an insular world. I was born in Moss Side, Manchester. I lived within the square of Broadfield Road, Great

Western Street, Princess Road and Claremont Road. All the houses were small, similar and nondescript. Every day I walked to school and back with my brothers.

That was my life, school and the journey to and from. It was the same route each day – no deviation. Not one of those houses had a garden, a tree, or even a shrub to break up the landscape.

It wasn't so interesting at home either. My parents worked long irregular hours and like so many families in those days we didn't own a car. Now and again we'd break out of the square and into the park opposite school. Going there was something of a fascination and a treat. There were play areas, grassy fields, tennis courts and a pond. There was fresh air and a sense of nature. I loved the park. It was a pleasant change from spending time at home and school. This was my life or so I believed. It was actually my experience of life so far because everything I knew and believed about life changed when I left primary school. I have no complaints about my life at home with my parents and three brothers. I could not say it was dull then because I had nothing to compare it with. Life was as it was and I accepted it.

At secondary school, my world expanded. Beyond Broadfield Road I took the bus three miles to Ardwick. The world seemed bigger than I imagined. There was a greater diversity of houses, gardens and landmarks. The areas had their own distinctive characteristics. The people were different too. The bus passed through the student zones at Manchester University and business areas towards the town centre. The university campus was impressive with its tall buildings and impressive names. The scientist Rutherford had split the atom there. It all sounded so exciting.

At secondary school, the children were different to my original friends from primary. They seemed to know a lot more. They had travelled in the UK and abroad. I felt a great sense of loss as I realised I was at an educational and experiential disadvantage. Here they were proffering opinions on France, Spain and Italy. The towns, the restaurants, and the foreign beaches sounded incredible while I was still dreaming of a day in Southport.

My new friends invited me to their homes and introduced me to the term, lifestyle. They had grand semi-detached houses with garages, gardens, lawnmowers, and bicycles. They slept in their own bedrooms with posters on the wall. They had stereo players and spotlights for their homework desk. Their dads worked in offices and held job titles like sales director, lawyer and doctor. My colleagues at school seemed motivated and were full of energy, ideas and opinions. They had expectations and aspirations. I had so little to say. I felt like I was ten miles behind with my thinking and my life experience. I knew that I had to change to be more like them and to become more competitive, but I didn't know-how.

I had grown up in a cultural vacuum. While my friends were talking about going to university and taking foreign holidays, I languished in the prison of a scarcity mindset. I observed for years my mum and dad living from day to day and from hand to mouth. They had survived the war with rationing and material shortage. Every day was potentially life or death during the war. All my grandparents had died long before I was born, presenting my parents with a devastating loss. They endured without plans, savings or a vision of the future. There were four young children to bring up and life was an obstacle course. When you're a child, have no income and no say in your life, you begin to feel like Cinderella. Everybody is pushing forward. The opportunities are out there, everybody is going to the ball but you're at home mopping the floor.

'Every person takes the limits of their own field of vision for the limits of the world.' – Arthur Schopenhauer

In 1973, my school announced that it was organising a three-week football trip to Canada the following summer. I didn't ask my parents for the £100 fee because it would upset them to say no. I was not known for my boldness in those days. I surprised myself when I signed up for the trip, although I alerted my teacher that I expected to struggle to make the payments. In my heart, I knew the dangers and consequences of making this commitment. To promise myself this adventure and fail would be unbearable, and yet it never occurred to me that I would fail.

Shortly afterwards, wonderful things began to happen. First, I received a 30% sponsorship from a philanthropic old boy at the school. The following week one of my cousins requested I work with him on Sunday afternoons at *The Daily Telegraph*. I now had a regular income to pay for the flight and raise spending money. This was a magical moment. I had broken the mould and taken decisive action. My experience of life should have changed from making that momentous decision. But my scarcity mindset dictated that it was a one off, a lucky break and that I didn't deserve it. The trip itself was a remarkable adventure in so many ways. It opened my eyes to the wonders of travel, the vastness of the world and the diversity of its inhabitants. When I returned home, I instinctively fell back into my default pattern of learned helplessness.

The sixth form was disastrous. I spent my time daydreaming and struggling to keep up with work. I complained of memory problems and learning difficulties. Things at home were difficult. A small house with four teenagers proved noisy, argumentative and awkward. There was no peace and nowhere to study. We always had guests and visitors and I continued to fall behind with my work. My A level results were disappointing and I continued to blame the world for my problems. I was asleep.

A pivotal decision was to start work in the Civil Service. I found the work dull, unimaginative and soul destroying. I was not the most motivated young man at this stage but I recognised early on that this was not the career for me. The upside of this role was that they sponsored me to re-sit my A levels and I grasped that option with both hands. Once I had passed my exams, I moved on to a career in IT which looked like an exciting prospect. It was the beginning of a world full of opportunities. I worked hard and put the hours in and I found myself in a niche role.

Now I was in demand. This was wonderful because I moved companies a few times and the telephone was constantly ringing from agencies. In 1987 I moved to London. I was going to be big in the City. The first three months excited me. Seduced by the money, the bright lights and the outrageous characters, there was no return. Then early in 1988 redundancy loomed. Even worse, my technology niche was obsolete. I was 30 years old and everything came to a crashing halt. Boom and bust!

CONSIDERATIONS

'It is important that you get clear for yourself that your only access to impacting life is action. The world does not care what you intend, how committed you are, how you feel or what you think, and certainly it has no interest in what you want and don't want. Take a look at life as it is lived and see for yourself that the world only moves for you when you act.' – Werner Erhard

Recently one of my mentors referred me to a social media guru. It was the right time for the business to become more visible. I needed to broadcast the message to a wider audience.

'Right Vince, let's talk about your email marketing campaign,' she said.

'I know all about email campaigns,' I replied.

'Fine, so let's talk about community building on Facebook.'

'I know all about community building.'

'Ok, so let's talk about Twitter and list building.'

'I know all about Twitter and list building.'

'Vince', she said, 'It's great that you know about these things, so do I have your permission to ask you a rather obvious question?'

'Of course. Fire away,' I said.

'What are you doing about it?'

That was the knockout blow. If I knew all that, why was I stalling on the action?

We carry a massive amount of knowledge around. But how do we leverage that knowledge? Are we taking responsibility for actions and outcomes? Or have we abdicated those issues because they're too complex or too time intensive?

There is usually a massive gap between what we know and what we think we know and that gap says beware. Mind the hidden traps. We're often paralysed in our thinking and afraid of taking the first step.

The same applies to public speaking. We observe speakers and hear many speeches. We have a general concept or intellectual understanding of what is necessary but that isn't the same as a practical, hands-on grasp. We're reluctant to take part. The unknown is frightening. Who knows what traps lie in wait? What if they ask questions that you can't answer? What if you're not smart enough? What if they see through the light blue suit, the false smile and the fragile veneer of normality? Ah, the shame of it all!

The question I like to ask in class is, 'What do you do when your car breaks down? Do we have any mechanics in the room?' Only a few hands go up. In my case, I lift the car bonnet and look down into the abyss of wires, connectors and sealed units. I recognise the engine block, the radiator and the battery but after that it becomes something of a blur. For the benefit of my wife and daughter I nod and say, 'Hmmm, best call the garage. I don't want to risk making things worse.' This is a coded message for I haven't got a clue. I know that if I put a lot of time and energy into becoming a mechanic, I am confident that I would become a good one. But there's no point in me investing years of time and energy in an activity from which there is no return on investment. Taking it to a trusted mechanic is a practical form of outsourcing and a sensible use of my time.

What I propose to do is look under the bonnet of public speaking. We can all identify the words, the body language and the tone of voice of any speaker. But for me the fascination is what's happening underneath the bonnet? What's occurring in your grey matter?

Almost every job description these days requires 'excellent communication skills.' You must be able to communicate effectively. You can try to outsource it, you can try to defer it, but one day you know it will return to bite you in the soft flesh.

Public speaking skills are a 21st-century prerequisite. In the online world, speeches and presentations are commonplace. Never before have we experienced this increased pressure for mastery. Conveying a consistent and coherent message is the order of the day. Now is the era of the small business owner, the entrepreneur and the solopreneur. We loved Steve Jobs and his presentations. Now with the explosive sales of smartphone cameras, every Tom, Dick and Harry has upped their game. Your bandwidth is bursting with educational-based marketing. Never before has our inner strength and mental resilience been so challenged to deliver top quality value. If you don't deliver often, your message is lost in the rest of the noise. There will be winners and losers, tears and champagne. So, make sure that you find yourself in the winners' enclosure.

'The best way to find yourself is in the service of others.' – Mahatma Gandhi

This book asks a lot of questions and points you in the direction of success. It taps into the real you. Your authenticity and drive demand that you make a bigger contribution to the people that you want to serve. In doing so, you become awakened to life's possibilities and opportunities. The phone rings inviting you to fly halfway around the world to speak at a prestigious event or deliver developmental projects to help NGOs in struggling third world countries. Perhaps you receive an invitation to speak to the students and faculty staff of Europe's equivalent of Harvard. Are you ready for this?

The secret to success rests between your ears. If you're not part of the learning revolution, there's still time to climb on board. If this book reawakens your passion for learning and your desire to succeed then it's a worthwhile investment. It's never too late to dive into life's golden river of learning. As my story unfolds, a key message is that it's not where you start, it's where you finish, and I'm not finished yet. More importantly, it's how you play the game, the action you take and the relationships you build along the way. No matter how far you've driven down the wrong road, it's never too late to turn back!

My principal assertion is that you already have what it takes to succeed. You are more than enough to survive and thrive in public speaking. To suggest that you're not would be to underestimate your capabilities as a human being.

'All that we are arises from our thoughts.' – The Buddha

When my daughter was two years old, I was lead judge in a speech contest in Canterbury. We had friends living there, so I arranged to drop off my family and head to the contest. We live in Bromley, south-east London, some sixty miles away. Throughout that long journey my daughter screamed and sobbed (she's not always screaming and sobbing) due to earache. As we left home my daughter was suffering, my wife was upset and it was my job to navigate the busy motorway above the backseat noise.

On arrival at our friends' home, my wife suggested that I dash into Canterbury, go to the chemists and return with some medicine. Great idea I thought, but the event starts in twenty minutes. My friends kindly volunteered to run my wife to the chemist and drop me at the event. When I arrived at the venue, my brain was frazzled and I felt like a selfish husband and a bad father. My friends were less than impressed as it looked like I was dumping my screaming baby on them. I wasn't too pleased with myself either. I didn't like that impression. I too had a terrible headache as my daughter's screaming was still echoing in the recesses of my mind.

I was about to push through the venue's door when I paused for a moment, closed my eyes, breathed and composed myself. I knew that if I arrived in a negative mindset my effectiveness would diminish and the pleasure of participation reduced. I have observed over many years that I am most effective when my mind and thoughts focus on one subject. When I am focused, there is nothing on my mind except that single important task.

Throughout the afternoon, my daughter's demeanour calmed as the medicine took hold. When I returned for dinner all was well. My wife, friends and daughter continued to speak to me and they said that their afternoon together was pleasurable once the drama ended. I felt bad that I had abandoned them to pursue my speaking engagement. For an afternoon, I felt like a neglectful father and husband. But I knew that that wasn't true. I would have opportunities to prove my caring nature each day going forward. It's easy to compartmentalise and rationalise behaviours especially when you have good intentions.

I remember the early days of fatherhood. I was often away from home and neither my wife nor daughter was well. I felt guilty for not being there but I knew I needed to be away from home. When class started, I had to focus on my students. At 5 pm, whatever issues had accrued throughout the day would receive my undivided attention.

The myth of multitasking – many people when questioned say that they are good at multitasking. When the definition for multitasking arises what usually ensues is a description of running multiple parallel tasks and projects. For example, while I am typing this manuscript, I also have three spreadsheets open as well as my email account. Every hour I check my email to see if any course bookings have arrived or if I need to respond to any queries. If bookings come in, I make updates to the appropriate database. I am also checking another database for an inquiry from my accountant about last quarter's figures. When I move between tasks, I feel that it slows progress. I have to refocus on the numbers, put myself in the right context and resolve the problem, or prepare the ground to do so. When I return to my writing, I have to reread the last few pages and pick up the thread. This is not multitasking because I can only focus on one issue at a time, whether that's for thirty seconds, a minute or two minutes.

When timesharing computers arrived in the 1960s, it was a massive breakthrough to have several processes sharing a Central Processing Unit. The CPU divided time into millisecond slots creating the illusion that many tasks were processing. It's an illusion because a CPU can only do one thing at any one time, no matter how fast the processing speed. These days you can have computers with multiple CPUs and attach virtual machines or containers to specific CPUs and prioritise separate work streams to make them run faster. The CPU can still process only one instruction at a time.

If you look at the number of people receiving fixed penalty fines for texting or using their mobiles while driving, you'll see what the authorities think about the myth of multitasking. Better still, attempt to multitask and see how you do. Make sure you're not doing anything dangerous when you try.

Supporting the underdog

In UK culture we love to support the underdog. The David versus Goliath metaphor applies to us all at one stage of our lives or another. We all have issues and challenges and the opposition can be the government, the courts or large corporations. They always appear to have the upper hand because of their structure, resources and desire to slow down progress. They try to use their size by making you feel insignificant.

There are sporting underdogs too. Every year non-league teams manage to beat their better equipped, better managed and better supported counterparts in the football league. Goals scored in victories over the top teams become the subject of sporting legend.

'The way you make me feel.' – Michael Jackson

In 2008, a journalist called John Sergeant entered the reality TV programme, 'Strictly Come Dancing' where a novice dancer is paired with a professional partner. It was a surprise to see a serious Westminster journalist participating on this programme. What later occurred produced one of the most memorable TV moments in many years. What was this man's motivation for participating? He was already a household name and an award-winning journalist. He had a first-class reputation.

I have no dancing prowess myself but I was certain from the outset that John Sergeant lacked all talent for dancing. He was awkward, stumbling and stepped all over his partner. To the chagrin of the judges and fellow dancers, the public voted in their millions for him to remain in the competition. We must remember that the premise of the contest is that of dance excellence.

So why did we take this awkward late middle-aged man to our hearts?

I can only answer for myself in view of what I saw and what I heard him and his partner discuss in interviews.

First of all, he was already famous, trusted and with a serious and critical intellect. He didn't need the money or the celebrity status. By appearing on this show, he put everything on the line for our entertainment. This man cannot dance and yet it never stopped him giving 100% effort every week. He had great connection and respect for his partner Kristina Rihanoff and the other contestants. Each time he was interviewed he made comments along the lines that he didn't mind spending 6-8 hours a day in the dance studio because he didn't want to let his partner down.

People loved his humility, his sense of humour, the respect and deference he showed to the rest of the team and how he put other people's needs and concerns first. Had he at any point taken himself seriously or exposed a damaged ego, the viewing audience's reaction would not have been so favourable.

In week ten, he stepped down from the competition because he felt that he was in danger of winning. Although he has a great sense of humour, he believed that would have been one joke too far.

In summary, he was detached from the outcome of winning and he didn't mind putting himself forward as the butt of the joke. He gave 100% every time he stepped on the dance floor and he showed great respect for his partner, the judges, contestants and audience. This is a winner's strategy as he will always receive the respect and support of others. People's emotion outstrips their logic. They wanted him to succeed because of his humility and how he made them feel.

Control

Hands up if you enjoy having no control in your life? As human beings, we love and fight for control. From our desired partner, home, car, clothes, hobbies, education, profession, we love to make the right choices that benefit us. We do not welcome anybody or anything standing in our way or interfering. When we lose control, we become anxious. We feel exposed, unprotected and we push back.

I cannot deny that I like control in all the categories described above. Yet, I look at where I started and I look at where I am now and I notice massive positive changes through times of stress and uncertainty. Appreciative of that remarkable process, I am now more educated, travelled and aware. I have made speeches to new audiences around the world and I have survived and grown stronger for the experience. Every time my career takes a new twist to deliver a new course, there is pain, a lack of control and also a delicious sense of excitement. I'm alive, I'm growing and developing. I have learned so much from my students. As Abraham Maslow would say, I am self-actualising. Thank heavens for the frontal lobes of the neocortex! I have developed coping strategies that help me plan, prepare and practice. Even if it all went wrong, I do not feel that my ego is on the line. I may have thought that many years ago, but I now know it is untrue.

Financial control – I must admit that this was one of the trickiest of all issues to manage. In my early freelance IT training days, I worked with two companies. Every quarter I received a schedule with the dates they wanted me to deliver classes. At first my diary looked full. I would be working two or three weeks of the month which was excellent. That rarely happened as they cancelled courses at short notice. Wanting to work and not working was frustrating. As time passed, those companies' education departments became outsourced and I never actually met the new training coordinators. It's difficult to maintain progressive working relationships with people you never meet. Then that company's education department lost its contract and it was all change again with little communication and mushroom management. It's difficult to plan ahead when you have no idea of what you will earn next week, next month or next year.

We all love control in our lives. It provides certainty that outcomes result in value and that they're in line with our expectations. If they were not, why would we bother in the first place? Control is good as it means that we waste less of that most valuable resource, our time. It means that we maintain open and progressive relationships with significant others. When we have control there is less about which to stress.

Successful people often make the rules and when you make the rules, you call the shots and you set the outcomes and expectations. You have control. Let's call these people category A people. Category A people, despite their much-deserved success become anxious when they can't set the rules or expected outcomes for public speaking and because of this they feel exposed. Successful people network with other successful people. Presenting to them is an ordeal because they perceive the success criteria are in the hands of others.

Category B people are every day, diligent and committed individuals going about their work, climbing that ladder to success. Category B people get anxious because not only do they not make the rules, they don't always know the rules which are subject to change at a moment's notice anyway. Nor do they always have access to the rule makers. If they did it seems like a good strategy to find out today's success criteria. Apply that to the world of public speaking and you have many reasons to become anxious as the likelihood of upsetting somebody influential in the audience increases. Stepping on somebody else's toes can cause trouble down the line. But, if your presentation is so watered down to try to please and appeal to everybody in the room, it's likely to contain little value. It will receive negative feedback either way. The good news and the bad news are that you'll never please everybody. Why not be yourself and say it the way you see it?

Lost in France – The 'What If dilemma' thinking trap.

I recently visited my brother's house near Falaise in France during the summer holidays. He has a lot of land and there is a catalogue of work required on those long summer days. Some are one-man jobs and others need group effort. I asked him for a list of garden priorities. He then told me when his family should arrive and we discussed shopping requirements. I told him that we would make a meal in anticipation of their arrival.

Control - a simple negotiation of outcomes and expectations. We all love control. It makes us feel secure as it builds and maintains relationships.

I have visited my brother's house in France for many years and here I am presenting an abridged version of events.

The first year we visited was more than a holiday, it was an adventure. I hadn't driven abroad for years so I had concerns about our safety. Arriving on the evening boat and driving in the dark was another issue as I had fitted the headlight adjusters and gathered the motoring paraphernalia required for France. The house is in the back of beyond, miles from the nearest town. Would we find it in the dark without satellite navigation?

The answer was no. We arrived at Falaise, a town steeped in history and currently under siege of unlit roundabouts. After thirty minutes of driving in circles I became frustrated. A quick call to my brother ended the magical mystery tour and he rescued us by the illuminated walls of William the Conqueror's castle.

The following day was rainy and blustery and I was still a little tired from the sea crossing. After breakfast we planned to visit a local flea market in Bazoche. With my brother and his wife on board, the holiday joy finally began. The journey ended some fifty yards later when the overloaded car ran over his gate post and ripped off part of the exhaust pipe. My Vauxhall Opel looked crestfallen standing in the mud and drizzle.

We spent an hour under the car inspecting the extent of the damage. It didn't look good. The pipe dangled to the ground and revealed a significant hole through which exhaust gases spluttered. The following day my brother towed me into Falaise where all but one of the garages was closed. We arrived at the main Renault dealership where they pronounced the requirement of a brand-new exhaust system. With parts, labour and delivery the bill came to £1500. But, because it was the middle of August, delivery would not take place until early September, two weeks after we were due to return to Calais.

After a little more exploration, we found a back-street garage in a local village where within minutes the mechanic affected an ingenious *provisoire*. Jean-Luc pulled out two wire coat hangers from a drawer and with a couple of twists from his rusty pliers, the job ended. The exhaust was working despite damage to the pipe. This short-term solution would see us back to London and last a month before it gave way to heat and vibration. Price - there was no price. The bar was open at 6 pm and if we wanted to buy him a drink... So, we arrived armed with a bottle of cognac.

The rest of the holiday went to plan and we made it back to Bromley without further incident. I was mindful that the exhaust could drop off at any time. Though I had foreign breakdown cover, one of my friends had experienced similar problems. Some years later, he was still receiving billing demands from the authorities.

Looking back on this adventure, I experienced heavy anxiety about my family's safety. Perhaps we would be stuck on the side of a motorway trying to contact French emergency services. I would feel guilty for putting them in unnecessary danger.

My brother pointed out that we should have taken the boat from Portsmouth. This is only a two-hour drive from Bromley to Portsmouth and then a 4.5 hours cruise to Ouistreham and a 45 minute drive to Falaise. But there are only three sailings per day, so we opted for the drive to Calais and then the 6 hour drive across northern France. It was an experiment and a new chapter of adventure in our French experience, or so we told ourselves. Without previous experience of this route we had no idea that the sailings were problematical. Nor that the drive, in high temperatures, would be quite so arduous. Nor did we understand that French service stations only opened for hot food at 12 noon and then closed two hours later. Driving without food was tough.

There were lots of good reasons why we took this trip. We love France, we love trying to improve our French and, of course, another visit to my brother's country house. I do things for positive reasons.

That said, there are always more reasons not to do anything and there are many people with negative mindsets trawling through their memory banks searching for those reasons to do nothing. Looking back on that adventure I could ask many 'What if' questions:

What if the car broke down?

What if it broke down on the motorway?

What I forgot to bring the boat tickets?

What if the service stations closed and I can't feed my family?

What if I had my foreign currency stolen?

What if I had an accident that involved the police?

What if I lost my passport, bags or credit card?

What if any one of us was ill?

None of those questions or their answers looks particularly appealing. If any of them happened, I'd see it as a major inconvenience except for the police option. If it involved missed sailings, rebooking, trips to the consulate, added expenses, business continuity issues, lost courses and revenue and the hiring of a lawyer then so be it. Whatever happened, I would have to manage the situation as it unfolded. Every one of those issues can be resolved in time. So long as I had not indulged in any criminal or reckless behaviour it would work out. Not much control to speak of although I would deal with all issues as and when they arose.

In my work there is a serious problem with the 'what if' question which usually follows this structure:

What if [condition] = catastrophic outcome?

This structure indicates that the student has issues with their beliefs around their ability to resolve the issue - compounding their belief in a lack of control.

The student already knows the answer to the question, so it's not actually a question. It's a trap which if pursued spirals down into further catastrophic scenarios and negative outcomes. If the student is already visualising a catastrophic outcome to their question then they're choosing to ignore the relevance of what's happening in class. They're already projecting future failure for themselves as they're ensnared in negative thinking. So how do we best manage 'what if' questions? The answer is to deal with it – whatever 'it' is. What if I had a panic attack on the London tube? Deal with it. Manage it. Seek help. The answer to all 'what if' questions are - deal with it!

That sounds a bit hard and uncaring. My point is that if you're not getting the outcomes you're looking for, please be open to listening and learning from those who have navigated their way successfully through these difficulties. The 'what if' question indicates that you're stuck in your belief system.

'Nothing changes but everything is different.' – Michael Neill

Let's start with a bold statement. 'We create our life experience moment to moment through our thinking.' Did you know that? It came as something of a shock to me too.

I was in my fifties when I found out. It was so obvious it was at the end of my nose. I never saw it. I was sleepwalking and then somebody turned on the lights. The realisation that life had presented me with a stunning illusion for fifty plus years floored me. It's no consolation to know that 99.9% of the world is oblivious to this fact. Knowing this secret has had a profound impact on my day to day life.

'We are never feeling our circumstances because we're always feeling our thinking moment to moment.' It's so easy for life to fool us. Throughout this book I'll present many examples of life's grand illusion. It looks so real and yet it's deceptive, and when the trick is revealed, we should be happy that it is only a trick. This knowledge will calm your mind and dissipate the gut-wrenching power of human emotions. Does this mean you become zombie like? Not at all. It means that you feel calmness. It allows you to focus more of your creative energy on the issues you want to explore. Life is a better experience without the weight of stressed shoulders. On the surface observe that the world looks the same even though everything is different.

Life's grand illusion

Some years ago, I attended (Christine) my niece's wedding in the Peak District. On the Friday before the ceremony we caught the train from Euston to Stoke-on-Trent and hired a car. The assistant at the car hire explained that her branch was closed on Sunday. She instructed me to drop the car at a Renault/Ford dealership some four miles away. She gave the address and postcode and reminded me that there was a £950 excess on my car insurance.

The weekend was brilliant. A memorable wedding and family celebration and later on Sunday afternoon we dropped the car back at the dealership as planned although there was a problem with the tail gate. It wouldn't lock. On Monday lunchtime I received a voicemail from the car hire telling me that the car was overdue, that I was no longer insured and that I should text them the location of the vehicle immediately.

At that moment I was eating a ham and cheese sandwich. My chest tightened and I started to choke. My mind drifted through disaster scenarios. The car was attacked, stolen perhaps and joy riders had run amok. My negative thoughts flowed freely. I felt miserable, nauseous and started sweating. I called the car hire company three times to update them but they were engaged. I was getting increasingly tense, angry and frustrated. Soon, they responded but I was unable to speak with the person who had left the message. Thirty minutes later I received a text telling me that it was all a mistake, a miscommunication their end.

So, what was I feeling? The car? No, it was 120 miles away. The dealership? Ditto. The thought that I had misappropriated a £20,000 vehicle? Or just my thinking in general? I wasn't feeling my circumstances, I was feeling my thinking. The moment I caught up with myself, the tightness in my chest fell away, I breathed easy and relaxed. Every thought has a preloaded emotion or feeling. The entire anxiety process is generated by thought and self-induced. The illusions that life projects are credible and impressive. They fooled me for over fifty years. Now I know that they're not real, I can see through the illusion.

Imagination

Exercise:

What happens when you imagine?

Have a pen and a piece of paper handy.

Imagine what it feels like when you think that you're an effective speaker.

Close your eyes. See yourself on stage delivering a speech or making a presentation and putting in a creditable performance. See your facial expressions; you're smiling and looking confident. Your voice is clear and you speak with conviction, warmth and clarity. The audience is buying into your message.

What do those thoughts do for you? How do they make you feel? What would those thoughts give you on a day to day basis? How would you feel if you knew that there was no failure? How would you feel if it was ok to fail? How would you feel if you knew that you didn't need the approval and appreciation of your audience?

Please do not continue until you've jotted down your answers.

There are many questions above. Please tell me that you're curious about the answers. Tell me that you'll give these questions (and their answers) the 100% opportunity to impact your life. If you don't, you'll have wasted your time and energy. Please give this exercise your full attention.

Did you know that your subconscious mind will spend ten to fifteen minutes trying to answer these questions anyway? Isn't that amazing? You're looking for answers and you're not even aware of it. And that's what we're going to explore in this section. That wonderful organ between your ears is your best friend. Even if sometimes it seems to have an existence of its own.

'The voice inside your head is not the voice of God, although it sounds like it thinks it is.' – Cheri Huber

In the summer of 2012, some terrible storms hit the UK. One weekend, my former colleague, Jeff came over from the New Forest with his wife and two children. We shared a cosy weekend despite the weather.

At 6 pm on Sunday evening the storm was lashing the south-east of England and I asked Jeff and his family to stay another night. The storm would calm and they'd travel home in the morning light. That wasn't possible because of the children's school routine. The weather was shocking and as Jeff pulled out of the drive, I felt awkward with the decision. The A3 and M3 are exposed and badly lit. The storm was strengthening. I asked him to text me on arrival. I am an optimistic man but an hour and a half into his journey I had this chronic sensation of doom. I saw Jeff's white Range Rover turned over in a ditch. Steam was gushing from the engine. The exhaust was torn off and the doors flung open. So, I texted him to see if they were fine. No response. I texted again every ten minutes for the next two hours. No response. There was still no message by midnight. I usually go to bed by at 10 pm but it was impossible as I was still visualising his car in a heap. It looked so real. I felt the tension in my stomach and chest; my breathing was shallow. I felt nauseous. At 1:30 am I received a text saying, 'Lovely weekend. Made it home safely. Long journey and many delays, trees down. Jeff'.

I can't remember the last time I smiled so much. I rarely punch the air or become animated over a text message. But it's a reminder that the imagination is so powerful. When your imagination creates thoughts, feelings and bodily responses so strong you're actually creating a new world inside your head. Have you ever read an epic book where you create the characters and the landscape in your mind's eye? It looks real, you can see it, you created it but it isn't real. It's a virtual creation. There you are reading in your living room, sitting on a sofa with a cup of tea and light streaming in through the window. Physically we reside in the world of form, the explicate order. Yet inside our heads there is another world, the implicate order; the formless world, of which our imagination and thoughts play the dominant role. Your thoughts are flexible, fluid and formless.

It's impossible for me to prove what I experienced with Jeff's story. There's no evidence, no audit trail, nothing. All I know is that it was real in the moment and that I can't prove it.

'Our deepest fear is not that we are inadequate. Our deepest fear is that we are powerful beyond measure. It is our light, not our darkness that most frightens us.' – Marianne Williamson

Here is a challenging question – who are you? Are you your clothes? Your car? Your house? Your job or your career? Are you your successes and achievements? Are you your friendships, your family, your Facebook, LinkedIn and Twitter accounts? Let me make it clear that I do not have any problems with the material or digital worlds. I enjoy the trappings of cars and boats, luxury apartments, foreign holidays, skiing and beach side villas (I only have a car and a small flat in London by the way)... Oh, and I like money. But these things can't give me what they can't give me. They can't give me happiness, peace of mind, wellbeing or security. I'll bet you know quite a few people who have material wealth and they are not so happy. I'll bet you know many people with few material possessions, some of whom are happy and some maybe not so happy. What am I getting at here? Your happiness, your security and sense of wellbeing come from within you 100% of the time. Not from your car or your bank balance. They come from your thoughts, moment to moment, they come from within you. They come from who you are. If I could use the example of Lady Di, there was a woman with riches, position, beauty and fame and was she happy? Look at the front page of any celebrity magazine. You'll see people who have every material trapping. So why are the same people addicted to drugs, drink and playing out painful public divorces? Ernest Hemingway's portrayal of life in 'To have and have not' tells us all we need to know about people's lives.

There are other ways that you can define yourself. When the doors are locked and you're home alone what do you believe? What do you believe about yourself? Who are you? What are you capable of? What are your motivations and inspirations? Did they show up in your life today? What would you do if you had a completely fresh start? Who and what has influenced you most in your work and life? What would you like to create? What is your biggest fear? If you spent a while thinking about the answers to these questions you start to connect with yourself at a deeper level. When you have a secure relationship with yourself, your relationships with friends, colleagues and clients also improves.

When you feel okay with yourself and who you are, you will realise that you don't need anything else to be happy. Material wealth or lack of it is no longer a consideration. It's the real you that matters – who you really are. When you're happy within yourself you can have anything you want. When you have that understanding, you become mentally 'bulletproof'. When you stand up to speak and you know who you are, the world may look the same and yet everything is different.

What does this have to do with you and public speaking? Perhaps we should ask that question to some of the greatest characters of the 20th-century. How would Martin Luther King Jnr define himself? Nelson Mandela? Winston Churchill? Gandhi? For these people, their sense of purpose was always bigger than themselves. Because of that they all faced their challenges and fears. They had the door slammed in their face many times. They fought against tyranny, bigotry, racism and ignorance and they won through. They had clarity of thought and clarity of purpose. Some came from comfortable backgrounds, some did not. What they were capable of was not dependent on their bank balance, their clothes or their car. It came from an inner strength and a burning desire for change and justice. It came from who they were and what they believed to be right. That property was emergent and I'm sure it came as a surprise to them as they grappled with issues that had a profound impact on the future of their countries and the world. They were role models for the highest levels of thinking and being. Their legacy long endures.

All their success was due to a sense of purpose, gratitude and a deep sense of connection with those they wanted to serve. These people were powerful beyond measure because of this ability. They often found themselves in unfamiliar territory. They were not afraid of the unknown, in fact they were fearless. They often collided head on with regimes. They all adopted their own version of Churchill's quotation, 'When the going gets tough, keep going.' What can we learn from them? We need to rise above ourselves. Our purpose has to be so strong that it will supersede the obstacles and tower above our ego.

My major point here is that you and I are made from exactly the same material. We all share the same DNA. What made them legends was always within them. Their greatness came from within and spilled over when the moment required. They had no idea it was there until these momentous situations arose. They had no idea that they would become legends. They were too busy delivering their promises to the world. They all had a sense of legacy for their nations. They all wanted social justice and because of that, they were like magnets for their countrymen.

'You ain't got nothing till you hit rock bottom.' – The Dandy
Warhols

In January 1996, I had travelled 24 hours by bus from Cuzco in Peru
to La Paz in Bolivia. When I arrived, I was exhausted, hungry and
grumpy. Bad timing too. I arrived on a Saturday during a
demonstration. The police were firing tear gas into the crowd. I came
for an adventure (and there was plenty of that), but I wasn't happy
with it. I wasn't getting off on adventure like I imagined. I was not
fulfilled by my travels. Two months into the trip and I had a terrible
sense of homesickness. I wanted to be back in Bromley reading the
newspapers and having a coffee at Henry's Bar. But that was just my
thinking. I was in a low mood and it's best not to make big decisions
when you're feeling low.

A few months later I was travelling in Venezuela. One morning it was
my intention to extend my holiday by a month and rebook my flight
home from Mexico. I was in a high and optimistic mood. So, I went
to the travel agent on the tube in Caracas carrying my passport, travel
tickets, cash and credit cards. Within thirty minutes I had lost
everything in a brilliantly choreographed mugging. A mugging so
good I never felt threatened or violated. To this day I have the
highest gratitude to those professional thieves' artistry. It was like a
magic trick. One moment the items were in my pocket, a moment
later my prized possessions had vanished. I kept spinning around
looking for the pickpocket. But no sign, everybody and everything
looked so normal. Surrounded by men and women in smart suits on
their way to work, I never felt a thing. Then it hit me. No passport,
no money, no tickets, no credit card. The police told me that I no
longer existed. And that is a strange sensation not to exist. It was
stunning. I had lost my identity.

Once the shock of the incident subsided, I felt joyous. I was alive! I had lost articles which I mistakenly thought defined me. But behind that at a practical level I realised that I represented so much more than money and a few documents. I wasn't a husband or a dad at that point, but the incident forced me to think about who I was. What I was doing and what I was trying to achieve. What was my purpose in being there?

The answer was simple. The purpose of being there helped me realise that all the material goals I'd been chasing over my lifetime were not going to bring me the happiness I was searching for. I realised that money, possession and adventure were not my true calling. I discovered that I was generally quite happy with myself. I realised that as diamonds go there were still many rough edges requiring attention. I had been looking outside of myself for the answers. But all the time the answer was within me, poorly connected to the source. This entire identity issue triggered a significant and ongoing interest in philosophy. If you're not asking the right questions the correct answers will always be elusive.

'95% of people experience life through the storm of their thoughts.' – Mark Twain

Have you ever had a bad day? You open your mail and your bank account is in the red, again. The relationship with your boss is a bit shaky since all the problems with your project emerged and you've been dropped from your local football team. Oh, and you haven't been invited to one of your colleague's stag weekends in Barcelona. Your brain feels like it's under siege. You are experiencing life through the lens of your circumstances and it's feeling heavy.

'In life you can make your decisions or let other people make those decisions for you. Being above the influence is about staying true to yourself and not letting people pressure you into being less than you.' – Anon

Imagine walking in the garden. It's a fine sunny day, quite warm and there's a lovely cooling breeze. You walk over to the shed and as you put the key in the lock you notice a caterpillar creeping along the door frame. Caterpillars are not the most attractive creatures, but it's interesting that most people will treat a caterpillar with kindness. We know that the caterpillar is in the early stages of its development and although we don't know what type of butterfly will emerge (unless you're an entomologist), you somehow feel a wonderful connection with its growth. If it were a wasp or a fly, you might be tempted to give it a swipe and dismiss it from your line of vision, but somehow you know that there's something remarkable about the evolutionary process of metamorphosis. So, you leave it and allow nature to take its course. You instinctively know that there's no need to try to protect the caterpillar. You just look on admiringly as it continues its remarkable journey.

In time the caterpillar becomes a chrysalis and through a remarkable transformation, a butterfly. I don't know about you, but most butterflies to me, look alike. Let's talk about red admirals, for example. They have a similar shape, size and markings and yet they are not alike at all. Just like you and I, they are unique. Each is a one-off just like a flake of snow. Each has unique attributes that make it special, valuable and worthy of life's respect. But it's not until the butterfly emerges from the chrysalis that it reveals its true identity.

Every student I work with arrives in the chrysalis stage. What will emerge, I do not yet know. But in my experience, every butterfly that spreads its wings in the classroom has energy, insight and a sense of emergent identity. I tap in to that individual's character, I tease out their deepest concerns and I reconnect them with their often-suppressed creativity.

'Get a second opinion.' – Vince Stevenson

If you are not an experienced speaker, do not be too harsh on yourself. You could be a good speaker but in some professional circles, your colleagues are unlikely to give you the credit you deserve. Where there are people there is politics. They don't want to encourage a talented colleague too much when there's a round of promotions coming up. In my experience, people can be less than objective and sometimes cruel by playing on the insecurities of younger and less experienced members of staff.

If your colleagues are unkind you may choose to believe them. If they convince you that you're struggling, that's what you'll tell yourself, and it will look like you're struggling. That's dangerous, but when it's so close to you, you just can't see it. Get a second opinion, because you can sell yourself anything.

'Objectivity is purely subjective.' – Woody Allen

It's difficult to be objective about our own abilities as a speaker. We can't possibly see ourselves as others do. To quote Clint Eastwood in the film *Dirty Harry*, 'Opinions are like arseholes. Everybody's got one.' And a multitude of opinions usually conflict.

A prime example of this is can be observed on 'Strictly Come Dancing'. The four judges have the best seats in the house. They're the closest to the action. They all observe the same routine and the comments usually go like this:

Bruno: Amazing, magical, inspiring. Diva diva diva!

Darcey: Real fire in your eyes Dario. I liked the flow, energy and continuity and that's a great frock Sarah. Good work.

Len: The tango is about passion. You were holding Sarah like she's an empty box of cornflakes.

Craig: Sloppy, pigeon-toed and immediately forgettable.

I'm teasing here, but I hope you see the general picture. There are four respected experts and four diverse opinions all derived from the same space, time and circumstances. Who is right? Well, they all are though they're all applying objective criteria from their own subjective perspective.

In May 2010 I was a judge at the English-Speaking Union's world student final. There were four other judges and we all voted for a different winner. Again, we all saw the same event from privileged seats and we all saw it quite differently despite all applying the same judging criteria.

My friend Jason is now a senior policeman in the Metropolitan Police in London. Some twenty years ago when he was on the beat, he attended a road traffic accident in Islington, north London. There had been a pile up at the Goswell Road intersection. Jason and his team took twelve witness statements and they were all different. What does this tell us?

'Reality is an illusion, albeit a persistent one.' – Albert Einstein

It tells us that if there are seven billion people on the planet, there are seven billion different simultaneous realities. As we saw above, even people sharing the same time, event and circumstances have a different perspective of that reality. So, who is right? We all are! We all own our personal reality and your reality is just as real and as valuable as anybody else's.

My suggestion is that if you want a professional opinion on your speaking standard, seek professional advice. If you were ill, you would go to the doctor. If there were something seriously wrong with you, you would be referred to a specialist. It's good to be in the hands of a respected practitioner. But some people self-diagnose both their health issues and speaking issues. If you take this route in either case, don't be surprised if you're not seeing things straight and needlessly suffering.

I can't do it and interior decorating

Whenever I hear the words, 'I can't do it!' I want to scream. Not because I'm annoyed with the student, but because I am still annoyed with myself. 'I can't do it!' was one of my favourite scripts. I grew up with so little expectation. If I couldn't do something, I'd just drop it and say, 'I can't do it!'

Now I know that the world has changed a lot in the last fifty years, but many years ago educational resources were both scarce and expensive. No Internet, no web forums, and no 'How to' videos on YouTube. I recount this to my daughter and she pulls her face as if I'm crazy. Indeed, it is unimaginable for her and the digital generation. I grew up in the era of outside toilets, tin baths and coal fires.

I remember finding myself stuck with algebra and geometry. I would put my pencil down and say, 'I can't do it!' We didn't have the money to go down to the bookshop and buy some SATs packs, so in many ways I became helpless. I lacked initiative and though I was clueless, I was happy.

The library was some distance away and the prospect of visiting alone wasn't an option. I was astonished by my classmates' ability to do their homework and return next day with the correct answers. I dreaded handing in my work. I was happy because I didn't feel responsible for my own learning and personal development. That was something that the world would put in to me when it got around to it. When you're stuck and you have no insights and no external resources, you're well and truly stuck. Now, I'm painting a picture here of the sixties and seventies and I admit that I was clueless about many things.

Times were different then. When I left school, it was easy to get a job. You could go to the Labour Exchange on a Friday and start a new job the following Monday. There were more jobs than people, and in those days, employers were only too happy to pay for your training to make you more productive. That was great as there was no pressure on me to spend my time and money on my personal development. This inveterate seed remained planted in my head until the late 1980s with catastrophic results. It was then as the recession bit hard that I found myself without a job for the first time. I was devoid of relevant business skills and holding a mortgage of £100,000 at 15% interest.

My dad told me that when you're decorating, the first thing you do is prepare. If you don't fill in the gaps and tidy the surfaces, it will look a mess. How right he was. I spent years papering over the cracks and now I found myself in a hole. I was ready for the scrap heap.

'Wake up!' – Anthony de Mello

A man knocks on his son's bedroom door and shouts, 'Wake up! You've got to go to school.'

His son replies, 'I hate school. The children laugh at me and call me names. The staff are horrible and ignore me, and the school dinners are disgusting.'

'I'm going to give you three reasons why you must go to school son. Firstly, it is your duty. Secondly, you're forty-five years old. And finally, you're the headmaster.'

While out of work, I finally awakened and began a personal learning renaissance. I am ashamed to say that I hadn't read a book since I left school. I hadn't invested a penny in my education believing that my employers would always look after me. The job for life mindset was replaced with downsizing, redundancy and despair. I could only blame myself. In my mid-twenties I regret saying ad nauseam, that 'You can't teach an old dog new tricks'. I was a lack of learning time-bomb and in the late eighties, I went off.

I went off all right. Every day I went down the library and trawled through the personal development sections looking for material on leadership, inspiration and thought management. I fell in love with the works of Edward de Bono, Peter Drucker and the smiling face of Les Brown, inviting me to 'Live my dreams'. I knew so little about business and the world in general. Though once I started reading, I soon began to close the gap. In the words of Anthony de Mello, 'I had been asleep and it was time for me to become awakened…' I was tiptoeing through life trying not to disturb anybody on the slow journey towards death.

I was changed by philosophy and the insights of poets. Every time I made a step forward, I had to sneak another peek because I would uncover a contradictory view. I needed role models and mentors and that made sense. Then I'd read quotes from Antonio Machado like, 'Traveler there is no path, the path is made by walking.' Sure, you've got to find your path to success and not follow somebody else's, and that made sense too. Everything made sense as I read it, but with often contradictory messages it created a paralysis around decision making?

Under the radar

'Success is not final and failure is not fatal.' – Winston Churchill

Public speaking is an intriguing aspect of the 21st-century business world. In corporate life, young people make progress by keeping their heads down and peddling like crazy. They put in the hours, learn 'corporate-speak' and remain determined to stay under the radar. To be accepted, you toe the line. The last thing you want is to become visible. Acceptance is one of society's most enticing drugs. Attention and appreciation come close behind. Who doesn't like approval, appreciation and attention? Acceptance in the corporate world is perpetuating the status quo. Even if people don't share the same views and values, they tend not to voice their opinions. The job is to keep peddling while others in the higher echelons of the company force the direction and beat the drum.

With the emergence of the entrepreneurial sector, thousands of people want to run their own businesses. And they don't want to run it along corporate lines because work-life balance is the key consideration. Entrepreneurs dream of 'the four-hour week' as set out by Tim Ferriss. In this sector, few people have a marketing budget never mind a marketing strategy. Because of this everybody has to become visible from day one. Public speaking is route one to visibility.

The complete entrepreneur's toolkit requires you to be a charismatic, dynamic and incredible communicator. You must inspire trust with those from whom you seek investment. You must inspire your team and your community with vision, integrity and great delivery. You must talk about difficulties, adversity and pain. You must show how you overcame obstacles and describe the lessons learned along the way. The story is one of falling and rising, and not tiring. The most important thing is to stay in the game. Enjoy every deserved moment of success and don't over react to the false dawns and the broken promises that could shatter your dreams.

Like most people, I grew up in the corporate sector worrying about my annual appraisal and covering my bottom. The last thing I wanted was to step away from activities I could achieve while sleepwalking. I did not want to draw undue attention to myself. I deemed creativity, invention and personality to be character flaws. To remain silent was an act of self-preservation. Under no circumstances would I question method or process.

The world has changed since the 1980s. The online revolution has fuelled a different style of business just as it breeds a different style of personality. All you need now is a garage, a website and wifi and you can start trading today. Barriers to small markets no longer exist. That said, to be successful online you have to create trust. As we will see when we address this issue with Aristotle's Rhetoric, trust is a basic human need. You would not buy a product or service from somebody whom you do not trust. Similarly, you would not buy an idea, a concept or a recommendation from somebody whom you knew to be shifty, unreliable or lacked integrity.

WHAT'S HAPPENING TO ME?

Fear and anxiety – a distinction

One of the major issues I work with is how to overcome public speaking anxiety. This issue affects people in different ways. I witness many manifestations of anxiety, and it is something of a slippery fish. The good news is that everybody can move forward by understanding what's happening in their head and their body a fraction of a second later.

First of all, it's important to recognise the distinction between fear and anxiety.

Fear is a natural evolutionary process designed to save your life. There are many books on the theme of fear and it's generally accepted that fear is a good thing. So, if a snarling tiger ran through your office, running at full speed in the opposite direction seems like a good strategy.

If I were to tell you that a snarling tiger would run through the office in the next few hours (and you don't fancy the thought of the confrontation), it would be your thoughts creating the anxiety. You were not born with anxiety and you still don't need fixing.

I recently worked with a man who was telling me that he couldn't sleep because of his anxiety of delivering a best man speech for his brother in six months' time. The event is long in the future and the happy couple didn't even have an agreed date or a venue.

So, anxiety is just thought. Anxiety is self-induced and thought generated. It's what we do to ourselves (and I have done this to myself many times because I believed in the illusion).

The agitation associated with anxiety is your inner wisdom telling you to back away from that thinking. If you're on a motorway and you get too close to the edge of the road, you'll feel and hear your tyres on the rumble strips. The rumble strips are there to indicate that you're getting too close. So, take note and get back to the centre of the lane. If you ignore the rumble strips and collide with the rails on the hard shoulder at high speed, that too is an indicator.

Your body has an inner wisdom – let me explain. If you're involved in an accident and cut your hands, arms, head or back, your body's wisdom will grow back the correct type of skin. It will send white blood cells to fight off infection and your skin will grow back in time. Your body is a self-correcting system. It is drawn to a natural equilibrium.

A car is not a self-correcting system. When you have a puncture, that tyre isn't going to fix itself. It requires external action. How much time and energy do you spend either consciously or unconsciously healing your body after an accident? Not a lot! Even if you're in a coma and you have suffered serious injuries the skin will recover in time without any external intervention. In hospital, expect the nurses to dress and clean the wound, but the healing process is internal.

Your mind too has an inner wisdom. The agitation of anxiety is telling you to drop that thought process. Back off. It is an indicator. So, follow your wisdom. Thoughts come and go, they are transient. When that thought pops to the forefront of your mind just accept that it is a thought, an electrical impulse. You don't have to follow it or invest in it. Let it go. Relinquish it. Notice how much easier it is to get on with your life without the stress and strain of errant thoughts.

The major issue with anxiety is that of control or the perception that you're unable to control outcomes. Have you ever sat a major exam where you knew that your planning, preparation and practice were insufficient? Knowing that, you might have to re-sit that exam which could lose you anywhere between six and twelve months. Imagine if you could not choose your job or career path. Imagine if you could not choose your life partner. Imagine that your bank account was cleaned out by cyber criminals. I have already mentioned considering asking somebody out on a date. Are you anxious? I hope so. The anxiety indicates that you care about the outcome. The fear of rejection is powerful. And what if that person says yes? You now have to worry about how the date will pan out. Where will you go? What will you wear? Will that person like you as much as you like them? There are no guarantees in life. Anxiety is wonderful in that it shows you that you're alive. Situation normal. There's nothing wrong with you. In the context of public speaking you care about the outcome, I hope. You want to make a good impression. Most importantly, you're not ill and you still don't need fixing.

The Basal Ganglia, Amygdala, Mind and Body

The basal ganglia are busy looking after habitual and procedural elements of everyday processing. How much time do you spend thinking about getting dressed? Have you ever put your shoes on before your socks? It's unlikely after the age of four. You know it's a pointless exercise unless you're doing it for comic effect. How about driving your car in well-known locations? You know every twist and turn of the roads and there are few surprises. It's almost as if you're on autopilot which is fine when you're getting dressed, but not so good for safety reasons when driving. It's the basal ganglia that's pulling the strings when you're in your comfort zone; it's casually rolling through familiar territory. In public speaking, there's a huge amount of habitual and procedural activities. Posture, body language, eye contact and tone of voice can be learnt with intelligent practice. Once you know what works, you don't need to worry about it again. That's great because then you can focus on your message.

The amygdala is part of the old reptilian brain which considers three main functions:

a) Can I eat it?

b) Can I have sex with it?

c) Is it going to kill me?

Let's take the example of a pigeon whose brain is the size of a pea and only has the three main drivers above to consider. The sun emerges and the pigeon wakes up in a tree. What is its first consideration? Well, I'm assuming that it's hungry because overnight it was busy roosting. So, it has to fly down to the ground to find food which is dangerous. The moment the pigeon is on the floor it recognises danger at every turn. There are dogs, cats and foxes on the ground. There are children, adults, cars, bicycles, scooters etc. That's why pigeons are looking over their shoulders and move briskly and somewhat agitatedly (when alone). Generally, every moment the pigeon is on the ground it's scanning the area for danger. Is 'it' going to kill me? Thankfully, man's brain has developed far beyond its original version.

Another function of the amygdala is to store negative memories indelibly and at the slightest challenge to your safety, activate. If you're of a certain age like me, you will have the memories of the deaths of JF Kennedy, Elvis Presley and John Lennon. You'll remember exactly where you were, who you were with and probably what you were doing. You'll also remember watching in horror as the Challenger Space Shuttle disintegrated a minute or so after take-off in 1986. You will also remember where you were and what you were doing during the 9/11 atrocity? It's interesting that we don't choose to remember these events. They are imprinted in our memory because the amygdala's job is to remind us of our ever-fragile presence on this planet. Our death could be a fraction of a moment away. The amygdala doesn't want us to forget that.

The Fight or Flight Response

The fight or flight response (sympathetic nervous system) is activated when the amygdala short-circuits the hippocampus by a fraction of a second and sends a signal through the central nervous system to the adrenal glands on top of your kidneys to release adrenaline into your blood stream. It will continue pumping adrenaline while that real physical threat endures. The body's natural reaction to a physical challenge is to start demonstrating the outward signs of panic; clammy hands, increased heartbeat, profuse sweating, a sense of nausea, tightness in the chest, trembling hands and knees... as most of your blood is drawn from the vital organs in the rib cage and intestines and redistributed to the arms and legs. The skin loses blood from its capillaries and the face looks white and your lips turn blue. The signal is run or fight. This reaction has been hardwired during millions of years of evolution. It's a defence mechanism and there's nothing wrong with you. Self-preservation is top priority – don't you think?

These physiological changes happen in a fraction of a second as receptor cells in the adrenal gland receive signals via neuropeptides. There are 150,000 bio-chemical reactions in your brain at any moment and these create subtle changes in your digestive, memory, learning and reproductive as well as other systems in your body. Have you ever noticed how the hairs on your arms and neck can rise sometimes when you walk into a cold room? It's part of the same mechanism working moment to moment in your mind and body.

The mind and the body are totally integrated which is not surprising considering we were all formed from a single cell. We have one brain, one central nervous system and one skeletal muscle that spans the entire body (although for identification purposes we tend to give them categories like calf, thigh and bicep muscles).

So, what's this got to do with public speaking? There is no physical threat with public speaking. Nobody ever died from making a speech or presentation. This indicates that the amygdala is working overtime to try and protect you. Anxiety hijacks your sympathetic nervous system and creates the symptoms of fight or flight. The major difference is that there's nowhere to run and nobody to fight. We often freeze like a rabbit in the headlights as the capillaries in the brain seize. This is where deep conscious breathing is invaluable. More to come on this in Part 2.

Think of a newborn baby for a few moments. Newborn babies will cry indefinitely if unattended. When the child needs any form of attention (warmth, company, milk), it can only communicate via its ability to cry. For a parent, it's difficult to identify the child's specific needs because there is something of a blur around the message sent. The amygdala is like the new born baby's cries. It's sending a blurred message. It's sending the only message it can because it's hardwired that way. Instead of managing real fight and flight responses its signal creates ripples of anxiety. Its intervention is triggering the physiological reactions of a panic attack and there's nowhere for you to go.

When do we need the amygdala? When there's a real physical threat. When do we need a windscreen wiper? When it's raining.

In the baby analogy and only in this analogy, we have to ignore the baby's cries. When the baby is ignored, it will stop crying because the situation is not real and there's nothing to respond to. If you indulge the baby (anxiety), it continually cries and the problem persists because you're investing in it emotionally. We have already talked about hijacked thoughts and feelings. It's okay to feel this way. It's the body's natural reaction and it is a sensation experienced by millions of people throughout the world on a daily basis. The good news is that it doesn't have to be this way.

How do we overcome it? First of all, start a conversation with yourself. Thank your mind and body for protecting you so well. But be firm with yourself around public speaking because you don't need that level of protection. There is no physical threat involved in speaking. Be calm and recognise that this reaction is normal. Accept that there are millions of people like trainers who overcame their speaking anxiety, perform to a high level each day and actually enjoy the experience. You will not die from speaking in public, but it is important that you know how and why the system works as it does.

According to medical research, the human body hasn't significantly changed these last 100,000 years. It's good news to know that if I met my distant relatives from a few thousand generations ago, they would look similar to me. What has changed in the last 100,000 years is the way that we live. Today is Saturday and I'm delivering a course on the fear of public speaking. My phone woke me up at 6.30 am. I shaved, showered and dressed. I had coffee and a croissant for breakfast. I left my centrally heated flat and walked down to the station, caught the train into central London and took the tube to Euston. Apart from the inconvenience of the rain and a minor delay on the train, life is a breeze.

At work, I meet eight students who had a similar morning experience. So, I ask them to imagine what would we have been doing 100,000 years ago? The regular answers are: hunting, gathering berries and nuts, collecting wood, making a fire and cooking, building and securing the shelter from predators, making clothes and tidying the cave. I then ask them to imagine the males in the group marching through the forest wearing their loin cloths and carrying spears and clubs. The group has been marching for ten minutes, checking traps and hunting for deer and wild boar. No luck so far. Then in the distance we hear the snarl of the sabre-tooth tiger, but it's a long way off. The sabre-tooth tiger is also hunting and has a voracious appetite for humans. It's strong, fast and agile. One swipe of its mighty claw can rip a man apart. It's a killing machine. Just hearing that snarl chills every fibre in your body. It would seem a sensible strategy to head back to the homestead, build up the fire and sharpen the spears. The amygdala has sensed danger and your body is reacting to the challenge. A jog back home seems like the appropriate decision. But when we're just 200 yards from the homestead we hear another sickening roar of the sabre-tooth tiger and this time it's about twenty yards away. You see the beast close up for the first time. It's huge and terrifying. Your body is consumed with fear – you're intensely excited. You're swimming in adrenaline. You need to run or fight. What is it to be?

Can you see how different life is now to then? We now have villages, towns and cities and the dangerous wild animals are either extinct or found in a zoo. What I didn't mention is that man was the top predator in those days. There was a scarcity of homesteads, food and I assume that every day was a test of survival. There were fierce local rivalries between tribes and settlements; regular violence, bloodletting and the stealing of land, crops and resources.

That said, we still need the amygdala. It plays a pivotal role in our everyday lives. Every time we cross a busy road the amygdala is on alert. Every time something unpleasant or unexpected happens the amygdala is tracking it for you. Ladies, have you ever got off the train late at night and walked home or to your car? During that walk did you ever feel that you could hear footsteps behind you? Did your heart start to race? Did you feel a sense of heightened awareness? The amygdala is your personal alarm system. Car and house alarms go off for no reason. It's a good insurance, but you only need it when you need it. The rest of the time it can get in the way.

Adrenaline

Have you ever booked a holiday online? It's great because the moment you hit send and pay for the flights and holiday, the internal debate is over. You're on your way. Those weeks of where will I go? What will I need? B&B, half-board, 3, 4 or 5 star hotel? Can I really afford this? The questions are answered and it's a wonderful feeling. Every moment of floating in that sensation is a heady almost intoxicating experience. Each time you consider any pleasurable aspect of the holiday you're sending a signal to the adrenal glands to release more adrenaline into the blood stream and when it hits your brain, boy you feel high. Your brain has a reward scheme and it's called dopamine. When we do anything that brings pleasure, dopamine is pushing you towards it. Adrenaline and dopamine are a compelling combination.

Now, earlier I was talking about adrenaline pumped into the blood stream and making you feel nervous, apprehensive or anxious. Am I talking about the same substance? Am I saying that adrenaline makes you feel high and the same substance makes you feel down?

That's exactly what I'm saying.

Adrenaline is a double-edged sword. There is no good adrenaline and there isn't bad adrenaline. There is just adrenaline.

So, what's the difference between the substance that makes you feel high and the substance that makes you feel low? There is a simple answer and that is how you perceive it in your brain. Either way, it's adrenaline, so you may as well make it work for you. When I speak, I feel a nervous excitement, just like when I was a footballer. I am on a high because I care about the outcome. It's adrenaline that fuels performance.

WHERE DO YOU FIND INSPIRATION?

I find my inspiration almost anywhere. I was just watching the news and meningitis was the theme. The article followed a four-year old girl who had suffered from an indiscriminate attack aged two. During the illness she lost both her hands. Yet there she was in a dance class with an enormous smile doing the same routine as the other children. After dancing it was lunchtime and we saw her helping herself to sandwiches and salad. She moved her forearms in pincer movements to get the food on the plate and then carry the plate balanced on her shoulders and arms back to her chair. There was no suggestion of pain or suffering. The focus was on moving forward. The focus was on what she could do, not the opposite. There was nothing this child or anybody could do about her past, she was only concerned for the now and her future. When I see children display such courage it makes me pause and I look at my own life day to day. My biggest problem this week was tube delays and organising my daughter's birthday party. In view of what I have just seen from this incredible child, I need to manage my impatience and petty frustrations better from now onwards.

Joaquin Rodrigo

Joaquin Rodrigo is Spain's most famous composer. The popularity of his 'Concierto de Aranjuez' placed him among the top tier of 20th-century composers. What most people do not know about Rodrigo was that from the age of three, he was almost completely blind after being struck by diphtheria. Such was his love for music he continued his passion for composing for the guitar without actually mastering the instrument himself. His compositions were transcribed from braille notation into musical notation for publication. He was a family man, happy and inspired to be able to follow his passion for music despite his difficulties. When he died in 1999, aged 97, he was one of Spain's most loved and celebrated personalities. The state bestowed upon him the highest individual honours available for his achievements. In 1991, he received the hereditary title of Marquis of the Gardens of Aranjuez. Although born in Valencia, his body was laid to rest in Aranjuez. At any time during his early life, Rodrigo could have said to his mum or dad, this is too difficult. I don't want to do it. Yet he did not. Who knows what the human spirit is capable of?

Early Vincent

I made my debut for the school football team aged nine as goalkeeper. This role was given to me for the simple reason that I was quite tall for my age, agile and brave beyond the limits of stupidity. I dreamed of winning, becoming a hero and holding court on my achievements. But the best made plans rarely work out. In the warm-up five minutes before the game I managed to dislocate two fingers in my right hand. Throughout the game I was in intense pain and dreading the ball coming near me. We lost 2-0. I cried all the way to the casualty department, partly because of the pain and partly because of the defeat. I was dreading going to school the next day. My dreams were crushed.

The following day I arrived at the school playground early and my friends were asking me about my bandaged fingers. They asked if I was in pain. Nobody seemed particularly bothered about the result. Indeed, I noticed that the children who were not in the team held me in high esteem because I was actually involved in the action and not watching from the side lines. This was a new experience and a new insight. People like people who do things. Anyone can be a pundit or an armchair critic. What the world needs is people who go out there, put their neck on the line and make things happen. Only people who make things happen get talked about. Only people who take risks get results. We won our next game 3-0. No breakages or bandages this time. There were lots of pats on the back but nothing significant in view of a 3-0 victory. Win or lose, the world continued spinning. Perhaps I was not as important as I thought. Perhaps I was not at the centre of the universe after all. Perhaps I was more important than that.

As a footballer, some weeks my team would win and some weeks we'd lose. Winning 10-0 didn't make me a hero and losing 10-0 didn't make me useless. What is most important is your personal contribution; your preparation, your desire to succeed, your technical prowess and your ability to adapt and master different and difficult conditions. You might also want to consider your ability to bring out the best in your team mates and create an environment of trust and support. In football, goals are conceded and golden opportunities to score are squandered. The blame game does nothing for team morale and nothing for personal growth. All that a manager can ask of any player is that we give it 100% each game. Your ego is only on the line if you put it there. Why would you put it on the line?

If you look at top footballers and ask them what's happening in their minds when they're playing, they will honestly answer, 'not a lot'. This is a great answer because it allows them to play their game (and it's the strength of their game that has made them successful in the first place). Ask a player who is under scrutiny from the press or from his manager about his performance and you'll receive a completely different response. When you go out to play and feel that every move, gesture and contribution is under the microscope, that's going to weigh on the mind. You need freedom to be yourself, do your thing and express yourself. If you go out there with a mental checklist and the objective of trying to please everybody – you will fail and that will create even more mental baggage next time. There is no script with football and the experience of playing is 100% dynamic. Everything that happens is based on fitness levels, instinct and the ability to read the game. Footballers need to play to their strengths during that ninety minutes otherwise they under perform.

Cricket was once my favourite summer game, at least for a few weeks in my last year of primary school. I was selected for the school team and in our first match I scored 8 of our 24 runs, not out – undefeated! We won and I was dubbed 'Slogger Stevenson' and boy did I enjoy the headlines and the bragging rights. The applause rang out around the assembly hall. 8 not out... I was walking on air. The next game I scored 4 runs, we managed to win so I was still on a high, even after this blip, 'Slogger Stevenson' retained his swagger. We lost the next game and I scored just 2 runs. The headline writers were sharpening their knives by now and looking for blood and results. Finally, and ignominiously in the last game I was out first ball and the team were all out for 5 runs. I felt sorry for the opposition. Friday's assembly was somewhat subdued. Where did it all go wrong? After my 8 not out, I did feel that I had to maintain that standard and to do it I was trying to smash every ball as hard as I could rather than playing each ball on its merits. If you're batting to protect your average and your reputation then you're not totally focused on the delivery of the ball which is speeding towards you. You will, as I did, get caught out.

In the business world, trainers are sometimes told to create a 'persona'. They have performance reviews with their managers who have rarely attended class with them. They often do not have the experience or technical savoir-faire to offer realistic feedback. This creates obstacles and contradictions in the mind of the trainer which are revealed in class. On the surface, your role as a speaker/trainer is to go out there and deliver education or training. If there's something else on your agenda like scoring higher marks with your students or trying to impress the boss for your next quarterly review, that could easily create an inner conflict.

It's difficult to play your authentic game when you're trying to tick other people's boxes and win their approval. The compromise is that you might have to give away a large part of yourself, your personality or your creativity to achieve those goals. This can leave you feeling empty or torn. Already, you're not looking forward to next week's class because you're unsure which part of you will show up and deliver.

Andy Murray – Wimbledon Champion

Was it not a wonderful experience to see Andy Murray win Wimbledon 2013? As a serious fan of UK tennis, I had never experienced a British player come close. Roger Taylor and Tim Henman always looked like they had the strokes and yet never made that final step.

Murray's rise to fame had tortuous moments where we thought this star would never shine. What we have learned from Andy Murray is tenacity, dedication and purpose. During his early career he was dogged by injury and bad press reviews. The press did not like him but he was just a child out there swimming with sharks. Imagine travelling the world alone as a teenager. Imagine the responsibility and expectation on his shoulders. Most teenagers struggle to get out of bed in the morning. Once he became part of an established team, he was taken seriously as a professional tennis player and his success is widely admired. He worked at his game both on and off the tennis court.

He developed a game plan for interviews which works well with the press, win or lose. All the injuries, put downs, lost matches and tournaments led him to a US Grand Slam victory, an Olympic Gold Medal, Davis Cup glory and two Wimbledon singles trophies. It took several years of fighting it out on court before he found that winning formula. Did he have doubts and concerns about whether he would take that final step into the record books? Of course he did. How many times have we seen him defeated, crushed and emotional? His progress is followed by millions of people and they (we) want him to be a winner. But we don't think any less of him when we see him lose because here's a man who is giving 100%. You can feel how much energy he's giving, win or lose and people respect that. And now it looks like a hip injury has brought an untimely end to his career. Life is cruel – but if you're not in it to win it, you'll never fulfil your true potential.

What has this got to do with public speaking? Well, in tennis, football, rugby and all competitive sports there are usually opponents trying to stop you winning. They can upset you, foul you, intimidate you, knock you out of your stride, abuse you. Even chess players of the '80s hired private detectives to dig the dirt on their opponent's mother to create negative headlines and land a psychological blow on the mind of their opponent. In the 2012 Olympic Games the French cycling team complained that the British team boasted a technological advantage. The British team responded by joking that their wheels were even more round than their competitors. The French seized on this (despite the British teams' bicycles being manufactured by a French company).

Mind games are for losers. When we're losing, it's easy to complain about the opposition and what they're doing. Analysing excellence is a good strategy. What can we learn from the opposition and how can we adopt and adapt their winning practices? When you're focusing on failure it's hard to achieve the outcomes you're looking for. As a speaker, we need to focus on our own planning, preparation and practice. Find your best message for that audience, work it well and deliver it with confidence. Stay away from the mind games and psychological banter of your competitors who will try to fill your mind with diversions and doubts. Just stand up there, be proud of who you are and what you are. The only thing that can obstruct you are your thoughts. You're more than enough for any audience. Even if it doesn't go as well as you hoped, it's a consolation that you don't have to discuss your performance live on TV with Sue Barker straight after an emotional defeat.

Titanium – copyright David Guetta – A song about resilience

You shout it loud
But I don't hear a word you say
You're talking loud, not saying much
I'm criticized, but all your bullets ricochet
You shoot me down, but I get up
I'm bulletproof.
Nothing to lose.
Fire away. Fire away.
Ricochet – you take your aim
Fire away. Fire away.
You shoot me down
But I won't fall
I am titanium
You shoot me down
But I won't fall
I am titanium
You shoot me down
But I won't fall
I am titanium

'Life is a contact sport.' – Sydney Banks

Football is a contact sport. One of its attractions is to be physical and impose yourself on your opponents. You have to be aggressive within the laws of the game. There are rules about what is fair and ethical and what is not. Every good football coach encourages you to play up to that line and heaven forbid if you don't. If you play a contact sport and you're not up for it, you're likely to get injured. I have seen people pull out of tackles. Get themselves into bad positions because they weren't committed and then visited them in hospital. If the adrenaline isn't coursing through your body when you're playing, something is wrong. If I ever felt low running out on to the pitch that would indicate that something wasn't quite right. If my mind wasn't on the boil it would have a negative impact on my presence. When you're playing a contact sport you need to be present and react dynamically to the play. If you're a boxer and you're not on the boil I suggest you stay at home and save yourself the bruises. We need adrenaline. My friend Robert, a parachute instructor says, 'Adrenaline equals performance', and I agree with that sentiment. You cannot get a peak performance state without it. He also quotes Anthony J D'Angelo in that 'the mind is like a parachute as it only works when it's open.'

In July 2012, we experienced the occasion of the London Olympic Games. Put yourself in the shoes of Jessica Ennis. Not only a wonderful athlete, role model and Olympic medal hopeful, she also became the 'face' of the games. Imagine the pressure on her as she came out for her first event. The hope and expectation on her shoulders was enormous and yet how did she perform? Was she nervous? Yes. Was she excited by the expectation and media interest? Yes. Did her fitness levels, mental strength and inner resilience give her an edge? Yes. Was she able to harness her adrenaline and make it work for her? Well we all know that she won the gold medal in the heptathlon. Adrenaline is a wonderful tool which is fuel for the mind and body. Adrenaline will either work for you or against you depending on your thinking. You're only ever a thought away from being on the correct path. If you jump out of a plane without a parachute, the only thing that can hurt you on the way down is a thought.

'Courage is the first of all human qualities because it guarantees all others.' – Winston Churchill

In 2007, I watched a documentary about the British troops in Iraq. They patrolled the streets of Basra, 'keeping the peace'. How about that for a job? Each day they faced the danger of guns, rifles and snipers, rocket-propelled grenades, road-side bombs, arson, riot and civil unrest. To me, that job looked like hell. Imagine those dangers each day on a foot patrol. It made me shiver just watching it from my living room. I have the greatest respect for their inner strength, resilience and dedication because I would never dream of doing that. Do you think these guys had reason to be nervous, apprehensive and fearful? I do. And that was the point of the documentary. It turned into a study of how each individual soldier managed and mentally prepared himself for the working day.

The documentary crew filmed only on the base as it was too dangerous on the streets. The men relaxed outside their dormitory in the sunshine. They cleaned their weapons and exercised while exchanging banter. Then they went inside to shower and rest. The most telling aspect of the documentary was the build up to their evening deployment. The chatter calmed. They became subdued and reflective and so began their daily ritual of mental preparation. Some soldiers waved away the camera, their faces glum and they refused to speak. Some were in sombre mood and offered monosyllabic answers. One guy was heard every night vomiting in the lavatory. These men shared the same circumstances and yet they all had different coping strategies. For those who were happy to speak, a common theme emerged. Although they all experienced the apprehension, nervousness and fear at different levels, their training, preparation and mutual support gave them the necessary skills to venture outside and perform their job to the highest professional level. One of them reported something extraordinary. As he took his turn and stepped out into the street, the fear dissipated and each forward step turned into courage.

Isn't it wonderful that nobody is shooting at us as we make our speech? Isn't it great that the vast majority of the audience want us to succeed? If these guys can face up to the torments of this hell-like experience every day, I think that we as speakers must find our sense of perspective. By that I mean, making a speech to a room full of suits in a plush office somewhere in the UK, isn't as frightening as the story we tell ourselves.

TOXIC GOALS

'The limits of my language are the limits of my world.' –
Ludwig Wittgenstein

I want to be perfect

Occasionally I watch TV. My wife and daughter enjoy cooking and home improvement programmes. I find the language they use shocking. "It's the perfect pie, with the perfect ingredients, grown in the perfect garden. The perfect house in which the perfect kitchen resides is no doubt in the perfect suburb of the perfect city. The pie will be eaten by perfect friends at a perfect dinner party..." Everything is just perfect...

This inflated language doesn't stop there. It's all too often found in the pages of self-help books which offer you the perfect system and the perfect results for your work/life balance. I don't think people offering perfect solutions are charlatans. They are just imprecise with their language. The net result is that people don't receive what they believe they were promised. This is not surprising because there is no subjective criteria for perfection (and if you say there is, I will disagree with you, because I can). People feel disappointed with the results. With inflated language like this it's inevitable. You should not offer people the impossible dream, no matter how well intentioned.

With 'perfect' language by implication you believe that if you deliver something that is not 'perfect' (whatever perfect is) you have failed. Your friends, family and colleagues will snigger behind your back. It's inevitable, isn't it?

My classes contain many perfectionists. I find it unhelpful that so many people should torture themselves because of a semantic misunderstanding. If dictionaries contain conflicting definitions of the word perfect, it would seem easy to misinterpret.

Perfection does not exist (in the subjective world) and it is the most subjective word in the dictionary. What is perfection? I once asked the class to write down their definition and then read them out. At my last seminar, I received 50 definitions and if I had 5000 in a seminar, I'd have 5000 definitions. What does this tell us? It tells us that if your goal is to be perfect, you are doomed to failure. If you make a little mistake, get caught up in your notes or drop your pen, that's not good enough. Students use this absolute language with themselves and it's all BS. Being the 'perfect' speaker also suggests that you can mindread the audience's subjective criteria for perfection too. I think that's highly improbable, don't you?

If you're caught in a trap, you have to recognise that you're first in a trap before you can escape. If your language snares you, recognise it for what it is and change your language. I ask the question, 'If you had a presentation next Wednesday and you were to deliver an effective presentation, would you be happy with that?' My students raise their hands. 'Does that seem like a more realistic goal? If that gave you peace of mind and a good night's sleep, would you accept it?' A calm falls over the class.

If your destination is perfection, you will never arrive. Your journey will be bumpy, anxious and never ending. Don't do it to yourself. It's damaging. It's so much better to introduce some principles and objective criteria early on. That way you have a destination and you can observe your progress along the path. So, mind your language.

Putting your ego to one side

Most people are not afraid of speaking, they're afraid of criticism. Somebody might say something along the lines that your speech wasn't so good. We're taught to be bright students, pass our exams and look professional (which are all sound pursuits). Then we have to stand up and speak to our peers and we realise that we are not who we think we are. We have a major chink in our armour. All the study and examination prowess doesn't prepare us for this situation. It looks like we're putting our egos on the line and that we are not the confident person we portray to colleagues. It looks like we're going to be found out. The infallible are not so infallible after all. What will people say when they realise that I am not 'perfect'? The fragile veneer is chipped. This is just a thought, not a truth. I empathise with my students. I am still a recovering speaker after all. I know what it's like to crash and burn.

"If your joy is derived from what society thinks of you, you're always going to be disappointed." – Madonna

Have you seen the movie *Mamma Mia!* with Meryl Streep, Pierce Brosnan and Colin Firth? Can those guys sing? It's not great, is it? Do you think they care? Do you actually care? Why would these Oscar winners put their artistic reputations on the line for our entertainment? They don't need the money or the publicity. What they needed was a challenge. Challenge is fun. Challenge is when we learn something useful about ourselves and who we really are. When we emerge from that experience, we are one step closer to realising our true human potential. Had Universal Studios employed some lesser names they would have sold about ten DVDs.

What I love about this movie is that these actors put their egos to one side and extend way beyond their comfort zone. They're not great singers and more importantly, it doesn't matter. When you see anybody stepping outside of themselves to deliver for others, most people feel great about the experience. Have you ever been to a school nativity play performed by eight-year-olds? It's wonderful, not because it runs smoothly. It's wonderful because of the missed lines, the amateur staging and the dish cloth headdresses. I find eight-year-olds wearing false beards hilarious. It's not about the performance it's about the harnessing of future potential.

Is it not wonderful that we give our children such latitude to grow? Is it not wonderful that we continue to love our children even when they fluff their lines? Why does that warmth and sense of nurturing seem to disappear somewhere between the ages of 16 and 21? Is it fair to expect inexperienced individuals to become the unassailable finished article? Give them, and yourself, a bit of latitude.

Our sense of expectation when projected on to the young and inexperienced is unreasonable. Without adequate training they are not ready for this situation. They take the spotlight and start shining it inwards on their perceived weaknesses. This is as unnecessary as it is unbearable. A rethink is required.

'Try not to become a man of success, but rather try to become a man of value.' – Albert Einstein

The objective of any speaker is to deliver value. Not to deliver encyclopaedic knowledge. Nor to try to impress. Nor to look a million dollars with your outfit nor to play the expert. The audience deserves something of value. Something that they can adopt, adapt and utilise from 5pm onwards. They want something that will bring them one step closer to resolving own issues. They want an elevated view on their current circumstances, perhaps a new direction. They want something to make them curious about an improved future.

I'm not good enough

If you believe that you're not good enough then you are correct. You are not good enough. Take the rest of your life off and I suggest that you remain silent as much as possible. Tiptoeing through life is all the rage, so you best get on with it. Shhh! Do it quietly.

If you're open to the suggestion that you are a proud sentient being, worthy of respect, worthy of an opinion based on experience derived from a life of study, enterprise and a few struggles along the way, welcome to my world. You have all the credentials to become an amazing speaker. Great speakers are not born. They develop in time. They are coached and nurtured. Each one of them has failed many times. They just didn't allow it to obscure their greater sense of purpose. The sun is always shining. Sometimes the clouds get in the way and we can't see it. But the sun is always there. Just like your personal strengths and your innate resilience.

It doesn't matter who you are and it doesn't matter where you're from, you have a story. You have a message that you can share with the world. You are a person of value, so get out there and give it your best shot. If you don't, you'll notice less experienced, less knowledgeable and less talented colleagues leapfrogging you on the corporate ladder. You'll encounter a sense of loss and emptiness knowing that you were in a race and that you didn't show up for. If that makes you feel bad, then that's good, because you can do this. And most importantly nobody else does it like you. So please, accept that we're all made of the same DNA. If the guy sitting next to you is a good speaker, you have everything he has. All that you need is within you. It's time to tune into the world's wavelength and start broadcasting. Be brave. Take courage. You can do it!

I want the audience to love me

There are some tricky issues raised with this toxic goal. First of all, how are you going to measure it? Is it the number of pats on the back, business cards exchanged, kisses or hugs? You tell me. I can guarantee that if this is your goal, you'll come away feeling worse than when you arrived. Frankly, your audience don't care. People are driven by self-interest. They are there and they're asking one question only, 'What's in it for me?' If you don't answer their question, rest assured that they will not love you. If your ego is fragile, I would suggest you find a better goal.

I want to speak like Obama

Obama is good. Some people say he's the best. I think he's great and I think that I too could be even better if I had a communications team of Harvard graduates behind me. As US President, every time he delivered a prepared speech, each word was checked for nuance by the majority of his staff. The President liked to get it right and so should we all. And would it not be fantastic if we could all employ such a talented team to research and prepare our speeches?

For mere mortals who are time and resources poor, we just have to get on with it. In my days in IT, I was often thrown in at the deep end. 'Hey Vince, we have some VIPs coming in. Could you give them an overview of project X?'

'Sure,' I would say. 'When are they coming, a couple of months?'

'No, no, no. About forty-five minutes or so.'

And that's the normal timescale in the corporate world where immediacy supersedes planning and common sense every time.

Do I want to speak like Obama? No! Do you want to speak like Obama? I would suggest 'not'. Can we learn a great deal from Obama? Yes! Observing effective speakers is a great strategy. Modelling effective behaviours is a useful shortcut to your own increased effectiveness. Observe Obama's pauses. Observe his self-deprecating humour. Observe his humility. He was a powerful president and he didn't ask for favours or make excuses. He just did it and did it extraordinary well.

So why would you want to be a second-rate Obama when you can be a first rate version of yourself? We only need one Obama and he's already got the job. Observe others, see how they make it work and ask the question, could I make it work for me? Always be yourself and always aim to be the best version of you.

It's good to note that in the autumn of 2011, Obama, in speaking terms became human. He was addressing Congress about the US debt crisis and he was umming and ahhing a lot, looking at the ceiling and he lacked conviction. Generally, he made millions of normal speakers feel good about themselves. You may also have seen the first of the 2012 Presidential debates. Most of the time he was on the ropes and looked hesitant in his answers and his body language. It was a great effort from the President to come back strong after that mauling. The message is simple. If it's ok for the then most powerful man in the world to have a bad day, cut yourself a little slack when you make the occasional mistake. You are not the centre of the universe and no matter how important you are (or you think you are), you're still made of flesh and blood. Give yourself permission to be human because, that's the best and simplest way to connect with your audience.

I want to make a fashion statement - I want people to recognise my beauty

A few years ago, I was working with an attractive lady in class. I knew she was attractive because every time she made a speech, she made the point of referring to her attractiveness. She wore designer clothes and had a classy hairstyle and I have to say she looked great. After exploring a diversity of speech topics, it was clear that she only felt comfortable speaking on two themes; how attractive she was and fashion. The world with all its wonders and woes had not crossed her mind and the real issue she came up against was relating to people who were not as attractive and as well dressed as herself.

If you have ever met me, you'll know that I am not the best dressed man in town (although much improved since I got married). And if you can bear to look at my face long enough, you'll notice that my nose is heading in three directions and I don't smile much because I lost teeth playing football.

Let me tell you that I do not spend any time worrying about my looks. I accept myself for what I am and who I am. I am ok with me. With regards to clothes, I remember my wedding day, traditionally a day of renewal. So, I bought a new suit, shirt, tie, shoes and socks. Then an hour before the ceremony, I put them on for the first time and how did I feel? I call it the big nothing. I didn't feel any different in those clothes. I was ok with me, excited about the ceremony and my marriage, but clothes are just clothes.

People don't attend my courses for my looks. Nor do they attend because they're curious about what I'm going to wear. They attend for one reason only and that's because they want to resolve their speaking issues. They want me to deliver substance and value. They demand something to take them closer to their personal goals. Can I suggest that when you embark with a realistic goal, your chances of achieving it are greatly improved?

I want to impress

As objectives go, this is a bad one. If trying to impress is the only thing on your mind, there's every chance you'll blow a gasket. What if you make a mistake or somebody walks in while you're in flow and you're distracted? What if you did everything right and you still don't get the outcome, the sale or the buy in from the key people you were trying to influence? I have seen good speakers turn their speaking into a performance. They put on an act because they feel that they are not enough. Have you ever tried to impress your date by putting on a show? I think they'd prefer to go out with the real you, the authentic you and not who you're pretending to be. It's difficult to buy into a performer because it's not real. If it's not genuine and I don't trust you then I'm not buying. Goodbye!

You will impress if you follow the techniques of effective speaking. The key distinction is that impressing is the derivative benefit of your extensive planning, preparation and practice. Impressing must never be the primary goal. Who doesn't want the plaudits and praise, the pats on the back and the kudos of doing a great job? It could result in a promotion, salary increases and greater career prospects. That will never happen until you begin to deliver value and substance. Always focus on the requirements of the audience. Relax and be yourself. Take your time and recognise that you are more than enough for any audience.

I want to be the expert

In 1992, I gave a one-hour technical presentation to some senior managers while working in the City of London. Following the event, I chatted with two executives from a large software company. They said they liked my style and asked if I had I considered becoming a full-time trainer. That gave me a lot of confidence. They gave me their business cards and suggested I gave them a call if I wanted to discuss it further. A few months down the line I was working as an associate trainer in their company. I moved from delivering one-hour presentations to delivering four and five day courses. Rather like fatherhood, nothing prepares you for these events.

This was like changing up from the 60 metres dash to running a marathon. My first four-day course was a baptism of fire, ignited by my bold assertion at the outset of the week, that I was a technical guru. Although there was an element of tongue in cheek humour, the students put me through the wringer. It was an uncomfortable ride and I realised there was a massive gap between what I knew and what I thought I knew. This signalled a return to the text books and weeks more midnight oil.

If you want to give the audience permission to dislike you, just tell them how good you are. They will tell you how good they think you are on the feedback sheets. If you set yourself up as the expert and you feel it's your job to impress them, you will find it exhausting and they will find you annoying. If they perceive you're doing this to bolster your ego, they will tap dance all over your self-esteem and find great delight in the process.

Empathy is the best policy. Walk a mile in your audience's shoes and you'll begin connecting with them at their emotional level from the first moment. I love talking about success and I'm also comfortable talking about screwing things up. It makes you look normal, real and trustworthy. Get your skeletons out and give them a good rattle. Have a good laugh at yourself. Take your work seriously, but do not take yourself seriously. If you give the impression that you're superior to your audience or that you're doing them a favour in being there, expect a negative reaction.

I work with many senior people in leading organisations. I recognise their career achievements and offer my appreciation in allowing me the opportunity to coach them. It creates a rapport by respecting their professionalism and in doing so, they're incredibly receptive to what I offer.

I want to control the audience

I was asked many times in class, "How do you control the audience?" To which I answer, "I don't!"

Of course, there are lots of things I want my students to do. I remind them that they're doing it for themselves and not for me, after all that's why they signed up for the session. I ask them to give me 100% concentration knowing my discussions and activities will help them in the short and long-term. Most importantly, I never tell my audience what to do or what to think. I always ask for their permission first. Sometimes quite explicitly at the outset of the day I make the point that I will be requesting their cooperation with many tasks. If they could help me with the logistics in the classroom and by giving me their full attention. I ask them to be punctual at breaks and lunch and to bring their professional skills to class. By saying these things explicitly, I am creating an environment where I am respecting their time and their positive outcomes. Running courses that last one to five days may seem like a long time span, but the days fly by. Managing time is a skill in its own right. There is a purpose behind what I do and how I do it – what's clear is that I can't do it on my own. I can only succeed with their cooperation. The more they contribute the more ownership they take of the process and they in return receive improved outcomes.

If you want your audience to dislike you, start giving them orders from the outset. Tell them what to do and what to think and then tell them that you're the expert (and that there's not much you don't know about your subject). Don't expect a hostile audience from then on, you should expect a non-existent audience. If you insult them, they will walk and then you've lost them for good, along with your reputation.

The points above are pretty obvious you might think, though not obvious enough for some people moving into the training arena. I have worked with subject matter experts whose approach sometimes is, "I'm the expert and you will listen. I demand that you listen!" If that's how you approach it, I would suggest that you buy a safety helmet. Or you can start classroom discussions, lead the conversation and guide it to where it's most needed and most valuable. Now is the time to recommend this, try that, could I suggest you adopt this, that or the other? Always leave adults in control. It's important that they remain comfortable in their thoughts and that they see, hear and feel that the benefits are within their reach. If the stretch is too much, they will never adopt the options you present to them.

In the next scenario let's talk about an audience of say 100 people. 100 is a nice round number and it's easy for me to work out the percentages.

10-15% of your audience will fall into this category

As your audience arrive in the room, many of them are distracted. They're distracted by text messages and emails on their mobile phone. They're distracted by being in a room where they don't want to be. Some attendees at presentations, seminars and conferences dread the thought of being there. They've been sent by their boss or a director and have no vested interest in your speech or its messages. They are in attendance physically but not mentally. They see themselves as prisoners of misfortune, victims of opportunity cost. They'll never get this time back and they can be waspish or dismissive because they're only there to show face. It's unlikely that they will remember you or the nature of your work. The only consolation to you as their speaker is that their lack of interest is neither your fault nor responsibility. That said, if you somehow managed to hook them into your speech, you could get them on side. If you're giving it 100% and you don't get that outcome with them, I repeat that that's not your fault. Perhaps nothing you do could bring them around.

10-15% of your audience will fall into this category

These people are glad to be in the room with you. Not because they're interested in you or your speech. They are so happy to be away from their desk for an hour. They don't like their job or their boss and it gives them a good reason to escape their usual routine. These people are often bright, motivated and open to learning. They don't want to completely waste an hour, they're just happy not to be at their desk. As the speaker, you have a great opportunity to capture their imagination and deliver great value.

About 10% of your audience will fall into this category

There are people in the room who are also distracted. They arrived looking forward to the speech and hoping to gain something valuable from the experience. But life is getting in the way. Their son is sick. They have forgotten to take their car in for its service or pay their car tax. They forgot to submit their weekly report by its deadline. They want to be there but they're distracted. I have more good news for you. Their state is not your fault. You will have experienced similar circumstances yourself. You're there in the room, but not there mentally. Distracted or not, the fact that they want to be there means that you have a greater opportunity to bring them on board. It can be done if you're skilful in your work.

For the terminally distracted, you must accept that there's little you can do other than arrive prepared and give it 100% of your professionalism. When you see somebody looking down into their phone don't feel downhearted that they're not giving you their undivided attention. They might just have sent one of your pearls of wisdom to thousands of their followers. Do not allow the distracted to distract you. The only time I intervene is if their behaviours were causing other members of the audience to lose out on their learning opportunity. When this happens, I pause and wait for the distraction to end. There's no point in getting upset or losing your rag. Wait until a semblance of order returns. Best not to make wisecracks at the expense of audience members no matter how disruptive the incident. Occasionally, the person or persons causing the distraction will leave the room and that's fine, because those that want to be with you 100% deserve that opportunity to listen. Remember that it's your desire to serve the audience and not yourself. Take your time. Do not feel rushed and the audience will perceive that you're in control (we've talked about perception and reality). We may not have much control over our circumstances though we do have control over how we choose to respond or react.

The rest of the audience want you to be fantastic

This category wants you to be fantastic. This appointment has been in their diary for a long time and they want you to deliver valuable content. They want to meet you in the flesh. These are the guys who make speaking a joy because they are there with their notepads and relish every sentence by absorbing your key messages. This is your true audience. These are your supporters. So, don't let them down!

'You are not who you think you are AND you are so much more.' – Addiction.com

I like this thought that you are not who you think you are and you are so much more. Why is that? My answer is simple – who knows what you are capable of? Who knows how you can impact the world? Perhaps you can't be a Richard Feynman or David Bohm, but who says so? That is a decision that only you can make.

On a sunny morning in May 2003 my daughter Natalia was born. The midwife passed her over and there was this wonderful bundle of pride and potential. She arrived, straight from the womb untouched by the world. Newborn babies, no disrespect to them, don't do much. They're excellent at pooing, puking and crying. They have an innate ability to awaken you moments after you fall asleep. They are not born with a manual although they arrive with a clean slate. Everything is possible.

Years later, I look at my daughter with a different sense of pride. She reads, writes and delights at mathematics. She's a fantastic dancer, swimmer and gymnast. She speaks English and Portuguese fluently and is excellent in Spanish. She plays the piano and the flute and she excels in all aspects of creativity. Who knows what she is capable of? Why not an Einstein? Why not a Beethoven or Da Vinci?

At the end of each term, my daughter's gymnastics group have a display event. Last time, my daughter and her group were doing back summersaults. I noticed a younger boy who looked about 8 years old. He was wearing thick framed spectacles of the milk bottle bottom variety. Instinctively, I was hoping this boy was going to do something less exacting. My heart was in my mouth when he took off and I couldn't bear to watch the landing. I closed my eyes and a moment later - thump. He landed squarely as planned, peeled away with a huge smile and returned to the back of the queue. He went on to do that six times in two minutes. My daughter tells me that he can't see the floor when he lands. I was humbled. Who on earth am I to dictate what somebody can and can't do? Where does he get the confidence to do that? That boy's human potential is incredible. But if you saw him walking down the road, you'd just see an eight-year old with thick spectacles. Who knows what he is capable of? It was a reminder for me to never underestimate anybody's capabilities. Have you ever talked yourself out of a great opportunity because you had self-limiting beliefs?

'The way you see people is the way you treat them, and the way you treat them is what they become.' – Johann Wolfgang von Goethe

When I meet with a client, I look into their eyes and I visualise them delivering a superb speech. I watch how they walk and how they smile. I watch how they stand and prepare to deliver their speech. I am sending them my energy and wishing them every success. Who knows what this student is capable of? They can achieve anything they want to. Everything they need is already within them. In the early days of my IT training, I made the mistake of underestimating my student's ability to learn. The mistake was thinking that they were as slow as I was at internalising new material. They probably found me distant and patronising. When you get it wrong, it's best to accept the mistake, apologise and move on. I had to wake up to people's incredible capabilities. In doing so I recognised that my job was to guide them, draw out their latent strengths and engage them in a discussion that made them curious about their emergent potential.

Speaking is not easy for the uninitiated. We stumble on the anxiety of the unknown. The mind or intellect is brilliant at working with shapes and forms but not so good with the formless aspect of thought. We live in the world of form, the explicate order (the physical world that we interact with), but it is our formless self (who we really are) that makes the difference. It's value that people truly desire. It's not how you look or how charismatic you are. Forget yourself – lose all semblance of yourself. Get out of your way. Stephen Hawking delivered great lectures because his only focus was the audience.

When I look back at my first speech in the mid-eighties, I recognise that I lacked experience and I was unprepared. I offered little value. When I look at myself now and the transformation I have undertaken in my personal and professional life, I'm glad that I sought superb mentors who tapped into my personality and authenticity. I feel happy in my own skin. I know who I am. I am okay with me. I have bad days and good days and most days are just great. I recognise that my life, my happiness and wellbeing are not dependent on my next speech, workshop or programme. All I have to do is turn up, give it 100% in the moment and I'm confident about the outcome. My potential is infinite, my life is not on the line and my sense of humour is always a flexible cushion if I hit the rails. Who I am is unassailable, bulletproof and not subject to the world of form. When the world of form tries to intimidate me, the stronger I rebound.

'The ability to perceive or think differently is more important than the knowledge gained.' – David Bohm

'You are not feeling your circumstances – you're feeling your thinking.' – Michael Neill

The weekend that Jeff came over, we stayed up to watch the movie *Training Day*. I love this film, it's one of my favourites and I have watched it several times. Jeff thought it was great, his wife said, "it was too violent" and wished she hadn't watched it before going to bed. My wife hadn't seen the film and subsequently didn't like it either. The characterisation and context were too strong. So, four people all in the same room, watching the same film, but each one of us experienced it differently. We're feeling our subjective thinking 100% of the time and never anything else. You're not afraid of what you think you're afraid of - you're afraid of what you think.

In the 2010 World Cup finals, Frank Lampard scored a great goal against Germany. The ball was two feet over the goal line but the referee waved play on. Sixty million Brits shouted "GOAL!" and eighty million Germans said, "Good effort, play to ze vistle". We all saw the same thing but there were so many different perceptions of the same event. Our thoughts create our reality moment to moment. If there's any doubts, we'll often see what we want to see. We'll create a memory in line with our values and then rationalise it.

'There is nothing either good or bad but thinking makes it so.'
– William Shakespeare

A few years ago, I opened an invitation telling me that my niece from Stockport was getting married. My wife and daughter were joyous, so happy with the news and the prospect of a family wedding. Then came the questions; what are the arrangements? Is it a church wedding? Where will the service take place? I was not so joyous, same circumstances but I was thinking, 'Phew… this is going to cost me.' Hotels, dresses, shoes, travel costs, wedding presents… Only joking, Christine and Andy, but had that invitation arrived in the early '90s during the recession, I can guarantee that those considerations would have seriously crossed my mind.

VISUALISATION

I think I mentioned that I was obsessed with football. Apart from school and football there was little excitement in my early life. Although I didn't go on to lift the FA Cup myself, I dreamt a lot. I was invited by so many others to celebrate that moment of sporting victory and raise the trophy. I also had dreams of scoring goals with diving headers, dragged from the muddy earth and being carried shoulder high by teammates.

In the summer, I was keen on cricket. I would walk down the corridor at school with an apple in my hand and then pretend to bowl an off-break. Although I didn't own a cricket bat, I would also practice blocking famous fast bowlers' efforts while demonstrating exquisite technique, supreme control and then look back at the bowler with my eyes asking him the question, 'Is that the best you can do?' Jeff Thomson and Dennis Lilley were sick of me. At that time, I had no idea that my actions would one day be codified as visualisation. My somewhat childish day dreaming all seemed so natural, sensible and joyous. After the actual game where I had performed an action that I had mentally rehearsed, my mind could not separate it from the mental rehearsal.

Visualisation is a technique used by top performers, athletes and artists for centuries, long before the science caught up with its effective usage. Close your eyes and observe yourself doing whatever it is you want to achieve. If you want to see yourself delivering a speech to your department of 100 people, visualise the room, the audience, yourself (and what you're wearing) and see, hear and feel the speech. How did it go? It sounds so silly and ridiculous that you wouldn't dream of wasting your time on this, would you? Well, I know that it works for me and it has worked for millions of others too. Now that you know about visualisation, try to resist it. It's not easy, is it?

Many years ago, I delivered an IT training session for the army in the Midlands. I was expecting a warm office somewhere in the countryside, not a frozen aeroplane hangar working with men in battledress calling me "Sir." It was the only time I had delivered training while wearing my overcoat. This scenario took me by surprise and after the initial shock I set about my work. A few months later when I went back, it all seemed quite normal. I could visualise the scene and I was mentally prepared. No shock to the system this time. My mind had reconciled that it was the norm and off we went.

I mentioned earlier about the science – here's how it works. The subconscious mind can't tell the difference between reality and your visualisation (whatever you put in your mind's eye). As you're visualising the scene your subconscious mind thinks it's real. So, my suggestion is that you see yourself delivering a sublime performance. You are calm, in control and you're having a conversation with your audience. This is a valuable experience for them. It works every time for public speakers so long as you do the planning, preparation and practice. The visualisation process helps you see yourself delivering the fruits of your labours.

In 2012, my dream of beating Usain Bolt in the Olympic 100 metres finals was scuppered by the following factors:

I hadn't attended a track session for 40 years. I have an arthritic hip and I am 5 kilos overweight. At my physical peak 40 years ago my best time for the 100 metres was 12.45. I didn't send the selection forms off to the British team.

Joking apart, my suggestion around visualisation and what is physically possible is important. If I couldn't run sub-10 seconds 40 years ago, no amount of visualisation is going to help me. Don't blame visualisation if you're not getting the results you want. Although I often run the mental video of my 100 metres victory in London, I struggle to get over the look of shock on Usain Bolt's face. He's still angry and wearing a scowl at the medal ceremony. "It's just a race Ussain, get over yourself," I tell him from the top of the podium.

I have a friend, Ted, who for many years has not looked after himself. He is overweight. He's had several doctors' appointments, referrals to weight specialists and he's not making any progress. He is now trying to visualise himself thin and yet refuses to change his lifestyle, maintain a balanced diet and exercise more. What is the problem here? Visualisation or behaviour? If you're looking for an excuse then we would have to blame visualisation. But in the real world you have to make a concerted effort around the physical aspects of life to derive the results. It is hard work, determination and a passion for your field of endeavour that will take you all the way to the top. Visualisation is an effective tool for getting you there and keeping you there, but you still have to do the hard yards.

But I know losers who visualise – that depends on your definition of a loser

In the Olympic 100 metres final, all eight competitors use visualisation techniques. There is only one champion. I think that if you're an Olympic athlete, you're a winner whatever happens. If you're an Olympic finalist, you've beaten 7 billion other people to earn your place in sporting history. Win or lose, you're an extraordinary human being, and your use of visualisation has supported you to the top. On the day, the best performers win the medals. If you're an Olympic finalist and don't win a medal and you tell yourself that you're a failure, then that looks true, but that's a label you've created for yourself. An average human being will be in awe of you, and if I ever had the pleasure of shaking an Olympian's hand, I would never forget it.

We'll talk more about visualisation later.

'There is only ever this moment. The present is all there is. The future and past are thought generated illusions. Illusions you only ever experience in the present.' – Jamie Smart

I was speaking with a client from the gaming industry a few years back. He told me about his mum and dad's financial difficulties twenty-five years ago. The stigma of homelessness has haunted him ever since. That was his 'reality' and he felt that he could never get over it. It's a powerful story and if you believe that story defines you then it defines you. That said, it's not going to help you now or in the future. There's little sympathy for coddling your past problems. People have their issues to manage.

Alternatively, you can utilise negative experiences as a springboard to a progressive future. I always look forward. I remember many gruesome points in my life where it would have been easy to give up. When you're looking forward to a progressive future the past has no pull. The past is not your reality. The past is the past. Your reality is happening right now in this moment. If it's a bad memory, acknowledge it and then let it go. You might never forget it, but if you assign a neutral emotion to that memory, then it's just another thought which will come and go. Its power over you is held in the emotional attachment you invest in it. The choice as always is yours. Detachment is the best policy. Drop it!

That's easy for me to say, "Drop it!" But it can be done. If we examine the lives of just a few famous names, we'll see that dropping it is the best choice. However horrific the experience, what you do with the now is in your hands. Look into the lives of Viktor Frankl, Mother Teresa and Oprah Winfrey and see what we can be learnt from their early life experiences.

I had a Skype call with a client recently who told me that he'll be making a best man speech in six months' time and he's already experiencing anxiety and sleepless nights. He describes himself as sweaty, voice croaking and he saw himself crumbling in front of a large audience. I repeat that this speech is six months away, it hasn't happened yet, so this is all happening in his thoughts. It's only coming from one place and that's from inside his head. These feelings of anxiety look real (but they're not), they are self-induced and thought generated.

I asked him to visualise a situation where he was at the wedding, making his speech and getting a warm response from his friends and family.

He said, "No", he couldn't visualise that scenario. He was not good at visualisation (his words) and that visualisation is a nonsense and really unhelpful at this moment in time.

As the conversation continued, he reiterated that he foresaw a disaster on the day. He saw himself sweating in front of 100 guests, choking on his words and dying on stage.

"Just a minute," I said. 'A moment ago, didn't you tell me that you can't visualise and that it's a nonsense and it's really unhelpful?'

There was a long silence.

"This is my reality," he said.

"I disagree," I said. "Your reality is that you're having a Skype call with me, right now, in this moment. This is your reality. Your negative outcome six months into the future is a thought generated illusion. It's what you're doing to yourself in your mind. You're experiencing a negative visualisation and you're torturing yourself?"

The subconscious mind can't tell the difference between reality and what you're visualising. He was creating/visualising a negative future outcome and experiencing it in the now. It demonstrates the power of visualisation.

You're not afraid of what you think you're afraid of. You're afraid of what you think.

Let's do an experiment. First of all, take a deep breath. Read this passage a couple of times and then close your eyes. I want you to imagine that you're on a beach. You're wearing your shorts (or bathing costume). You're covered in factor 50 suntan lotion and you're wearing your designer sunglasses and feeling rather good. There's a cool refreshing breeze. You're resting under a palm tree and reading a glossy magazine. The sun is high and strong and you look out across the beach to the horizon where a deep blue sea meets a powder blue sky. Now breathe deeply again. Relax and enjoy the beach scene. As each wave crashes in take a deep breath and as that wave recedes, breathe out. Align your breathing with the rhythm of the waves. Oh, and relax.

That exercise is easy for most people.

Next exercise: I want you to imagine that you're attending a wedding. Picture in your mind's eye the bride and groom. The bride's dress is sensational and her father's face brims with pride. Then add the bridesmaids in pink dresses and the page boy, aged 4, looking cute with his oiled hair. After the ceremony you're standing outside the church. The bells ring loud, everybody's excited and the confetti is flying. You're surrounded by family and friends. There's a wonderful sense of joy and togetherness. Close your eyes for a few moments and run that scene through your head a few times. Are you there? If you've been to a church wedding before, that's a relatively straightforward exercise.

Let's glance back at the two scenarios outlined. You had a vision of a beach scene and a wedding. Did you notice how effortless it was for your mind to shift from one scene to the next? You created those scenes almost effortlessly. You shifted between the scenes and I hope you now recognise that you are not your thoughts (your thoughts came from my suggestions). You do not own your thoughts (they are ephemeral) and that you are merely the creator of your thoughts. Your thoughts are fluid, flexible and formless. Because they have no form, they can take any shape. You get to choose what you think about moment to moment. You are responsible for that decision.

If I asked you to show me your thoughts, you couldn't. There's no audit trail and even if you chose to write them down, they're not your 'real' thoughts with all the colour and imagination your mind's eye creates. Your thoughts exist in waves – brain waves. They manifest when you pull them from the hard disk of your subconscious mind into the RAM of your mind's eye and then they're released. They're transient. They come and go - in waves.

If you're looking for an external solution to an internal problem, you're looking in the wrong place.

'The secret to success is hard work and intelligent practice.' – Shakira

When I first moved into corporate training, I realised that there were many ways and opportunities for me to improve myself. I spent every spare moment on self-development courses, technical courses (the material I was delivering), and networking with other trainers to find out as many of their success secrets as possible. In the first year my student feedback was quite patchy. Some weeks I received great marks and other weeks it was suboptimal. It took me a long time to work out why there was such an inconsistency.

Some of the material I was teaching was quite new to me so I only had a theoretical grasp of it. It's difficult to speak with conviction about heavy technical material when you have limited classroom experience. So, I adopted the classroom discussion technique to draw out the students' knowledge. This worked well and after a few deliveries I was able to introduce their experiences into my classroom discussions (as I had gone away and worked through those scenarios and knew the outcomes).

Students loved talking about their work and it was a technique I used in other areas even though I had my own experience of the subject matter. Students' contributions in class became the most effective method of engagement. If they had little or no experience on a particular item, I would lead the delivery of the new material.

This opportunity to engage changed my approach to training. I believed that I should speak from the front of the class which is normal. Whereas drawing out the students' knowledge and building upon it worked more effectively with motivated technicians. I was surprised with the rate of improvement especially in my second year. Now I was much more confident, I had a bag full of successful techniques and strategies that I could deploy. I had dropped the 'guru tag' and my consistency as a technical trainer was beginning to win more influential friends in the industry. They say that you become like the people you hang out with. I only hung out with the best trainers and I began to learn the valuable skill of intense listening.

'The best time to plant a tree was 20 years ago. The second best time is now.' – Chinese Proverb

In my garden there's an oak tree and it's about twenty-five yards high. It's impressive and imposing. Have you noticed that we tend only to recognise the 'tall and impressive'? There's a smaller one too at the rear of the garden. Although it's there, it just blends in with the rest of the greenery. Within an acorn, the DNA is encoded to be tall, strong and have the presence of the tree in my garden. But not all oak trees are as tall or impressive. Why is that? The acorns look the same and inside they contain the same genetic material. The answer is that some acorns fall on good soil, some are well watered and some have more access to sunshine. There are a hundred other variables involved in the growing of an oak tree. But, tall or short, broad or narrow, all trees play an important role in making a significant contribution to the world's oxygen.

It's the same for human beings. You may have noticed that although as a race we share the same DNA, we are different colours, heights and shapes. We are born to different families in different parts of the world with different religions. We are from cultures with different educational systems, teachers and political systems and problems and opportunities. Who is more impressive, Mother Teresa or Barack Obama? Napoleon Bonaparte or Elvis Presley? You, your mum or dad or the man who invented the printing press? You may not be a big name and that doesn't actually matter because every human being makes a significant and enduring contribution to the world. It may not seem like it some days, especially when we're in a low mood. So never underestimate your role in the big scheme of life. We're all providing support to other human beings whether we work in a hospital, a car factory or working a checkout at the supermarket. We're all significant cogs in the process. You were born of the same material of every famous person who has walked this earth and you are just as valuable. There are millions of unsung heroes whose contribution to the lives of others is breath taking. If you're not one already, you can become one the moment you step out of your head and make somebody else's world a happier or better place. Now is a good time to make a difference.

Metaphors, Analogies and Affirmations

Camel Traders – Anthony de Mello

Along the way a camel trader buys a young, strong and expensive rare-breed camel. He realises he will have to make a new tether to secure the beast in the desert overnight. He is particularly delighted about this camel. He is impressed by its noble features, its physical presence and its unique colour. He thinks it will make a great present for the wife of a business partner. Yet he becomes distracted by more passing trade and the thrill of counting his gold coins. He then has to erect his tent for the evening as well as secure the tethers for his existing stock of twenty camels. When all his daily duties are finished, he realises that he did not make the tether for the new camel. By now, all his tools are stored away and rather than open them up and start his important project, he pours himself a tea, rolls out his rug and prays. "Oh Lord, you know I am a good man, a diligent man and a fair and loving man. Today I bought a beautiful camel and tonight through no fault of my own, I have no means of securing it. If I lose it in the desert, I will be disappointed. I have long desired to own such a camel and now you have granted my wish I fear that I may lose it. Oh Lord, can I leave the safety and security of this prized beast in your loving and generous care for this one night?"

The camel trader had barely finished his question when a bolt of lightning strikes the tent. From behind a puff of smoke his God appeared to him and says, "Do not ask God to do what you would not do for yourself!"

Sometimes we get lazy and take the easy path. We want the prizes but we don't enjoy the hard work that goes with it. Taking easy options is the express route to the bottom. What must be done must be done. There are no shortcuts. Be prepared to take responsibility and commit time to your tasks as they define your future success. If you have ever blamed anybody else for your lack of success, can I suggest that you think again?

Role models and childhood inspiration

In 1967, the year after England's football World Cup victory my school received a visit from one of the winning team. Nobby Stiles played for Manchester United. I recollect being in the playground on a hot sunny day having my picture taken with a national hero. I had the privilege of holding a World Cup winner's medal. You can imagine the impact this had on a football crazy nine year old. I remember how motivational I found that experience. I went home telling my family that I had met Nobby Stiles and my friends were so jealous. I felt rather special and my next football training session was all the more exciting for it. Mr Smythe our football teacher alluded to the visit for the entire last year in primary school. When I went to secondary school I was still buzzing with the story.

As a young man, my dad didn't have a car and I remember sitting in the back yard (we didn't have a garden either) visualising changing car gears for my driving lessons. Foot down on the clutch and into first gear. Foot off the clutch slowly and down on the accelerator. Drive ten yards. Repeat this sequence three times until you come to a junction. Stop and then start it all again. Visualisation and repetition are two of the greatest techniques in mastering any skill. See yourself doing what needs to be done. Then ask the question of each action – why am I doing this? How does it integrate with everything else? When you understand each movement and how it fits into the activity you will have a working model as well as success criteria. What starts off as clunky disparate techniques quickly become integrated behaviours that gather momentum. Isn't that what you want? I hope so, because the role of the basal ganglia is to manage such procedural and habitual activities. Your brain attributes a great deal of resources to your success so long as you practice what works effectively. The capability is built in to you.

The major point I want to make about visualisation is that we seem do it naturally. However, there are many excellent books on visualisation that guided me through the process. Remember that the subconscious mind reacts with visual stimuli and it cannot tell the difference between reality and what you visualise. Visualise yourself saying the right thing at the right time, most of the time. Then wait to receive encouraging feedback.

Stories, anecdotes, case studies and metaphors are all visual in nature. That's why they work so well in helping students see their issues from a different perspective. It's also why they should be used extensively in speeches and presentations as you want the audience to see what you're saying. In doing so you will become more persuasive because the audience will see your evidence and it's easier for them to remember. You will have greater impact and influence by deploying these techniques.

'We are only ever one thought away from the resolution to any problem.' – William James

I was recently co-hosting an event in Transylvania where I delivered a session on relaxation, meditation and visualisation. The venue was a hotel within a large pine forest on the outskirts of Sibiu. The weather was hot but down on the forest floor it was cool in the shade. It seemed appropriate that we make the most of the outdoor facilities. The following evening, we all had speeches to deliver at a formal group session in the city centre. I asked the group to focus on their theme for the speech and then concentrate on their speech opening. How were they going to open with impact? How were they going to grab the audience's attention and maintain it? So, we all made notes and mentally rehearsed the openings of our speeches. The feedback from my nervous and novice students was that because they had planned how to open with impact, they were feeling more relaxed. We followed this with a short practical session on delivering objective, supportive and constructive feedback on their opening statements. If you can exude confidence and deliver value when you speak to any audience, you will be recognised as a competent communicator.

Cars

Have you ever weighed up the responsibility of driving on the roads in England? Have you seen the statistics for deaths and injuries? If you did, you might consider the alternatives. It's much safer after all.

I want you to imagine that you're playing a computer game. You're driving a one-ton guided missile. You're given a steering wheel, a gearbox and a few pedals. Your missile is loaded with several gallons of combustible fuel. You're allowed to invite your friends, family and colleagues as passengers. The game is to avoid killing or injuring other road users. Avoiding collisions with other vehicles wins points. There are many rules like driving on the left, stopping at STOP signs and giving way to traffic coming from the right. You have to recognise speed limits for when you're driving in town, in the country or on the motorway. Depending on where you're driving in the world, the rules change. You have to drive on the right and most of the traffic signs are in a foreign language. If you're driving in a new country that you've never visited there are a million or so new variables. Every road, every twist and turn are either a new adventure or a torturous experience, depending on how you see it.

If I had to read the rules of that game, I would get so bored, so quickly, I would choose not to play.

Have you ever read the instructions to a board game like Monopoly? I hope not. It's so much easier to play by watching and doing. Take a few rounds where you test out the rules across the board, and then reach the point where you want to play for real. It's so much easier and more fun to learn something experiential.

How many of you feel comfortable behind the wheel of a car? Most of you? Those that don't, I'm assuming that you haven't passed your test yet. But pass your test you will. And I say that in all confidence that everybody who is intent on passing their driving test, will in fact pass.

You'll persevere. You'll study. You'll practice your driving lessons and you'll do whatever it takes, because I don't have to sell you the concept of freedom that passing your driving test brings. You know that when you have your car, you can drive anywhere you want, when you want with whomever you want. You can taste the freedom. Look at your friends, family and colleagues who drive. It's so cool and confident when they say, 'I'll pick you up at 7.30 pm.'

Everybody gets that fact that you have to study and practice with driving. It's important that we apply the same principle to speaking. You're not going to understand the complexity at a moment's notice, though it is important to understand the basics. With driving you utilise hand-eye and leg coordination. Your brain is processing vision, sound and distance moment to moment and in busy traffic with multiple lanes there's a lot happening. At first, it's quite intimidating. Those lorries and vans seem to come closer and closer. They seem hostile and yet they're not.

Theoretically, The Highway Code is a great companion, but it's not a friend you can turn to when you're in the wrong lane in a busy one-way system and nobody is letting you out. It's a learning experience. Go around the loop and ensure that you emerge in the correct lane. Painful I know, and once it's done it's done. You'll remember next time too. We make mistakes and we learn and we learn and we continue to learn. Remember you're driving a ton of iron with several gallons of fuel. That's a massive responsibility we undertake every day and we undertake it willingly and we put our children in the back seat, sing with the radio, light a cigarette, send text messages and argue with our partners about what we're having for dinner. (Leave the cigarettes and mobile phone in the glove compartment.)

After a while being in the wrong lane doesn't seem quite so intimidating. Let people honk their horns and make obscene gestures. They'll get over it and so will you. And no matter how good a driver you become you will still make mistakes. Life and the world will continue whatever happens. You're not as important or as fragile as you may think you are (that goes for me too). And most importantly, it won't stop you wanting to do what you want to do when you want to do it.

Affirmations – I'm ok - stay ok

I've never been one for affirmations. I prefer quotations as they make you ponder, think and reflect. They're not absolute truths. They're subjective entities that point you in the right direction. Affirmations are used for creating a positive line of communication between you and what you want to achieve. 'I can do it' is a good affirmation.

Many years ago, I read a book called *I'm ok – You're ok* by Thomas A Harris MD. I don't remember all the detail, but I do remember the one major point that stayed with me, and that was that I have always felt that as a person, I'm okay.

By that I mean I'm not useless (although I could always be better) and there is nothing outstanding about me (although that's not true either, I am exceptional at some things). On a day to day basis I feel okay. Some days I do the most wonderful things; deliver great classes, win bids and contracts and take my daughter to new activities and adventures. I love days like that and when it happens and when it's happening, I'm okay. Some days it doesn't go so well. I have Internet access problems, telephonic problems (bad reception or noise pollution). Or a disagreement with my wife or daughter and I think that's just part of everyday life. Things will self-correct and return to normal and I'm okay with that too.

I set high expectations for myself. If I'm not in class or working with a client I'm reading a self-development book or listening to an audio or writing a book or preparing a lesson. When I'm involved in productive activities, I'm okay. If I'm hanging on the line speaking to a call centre who are reluctant to help me, I'm not okay and I think about the wasted time and what it's cost me. After a short while of reflective thinking my mind self-corrects and I'm okay again.

When I'm okay, things happen, my mind shifts and mountains move. When I'm okay I make good decisions, my mind and my thinking are balanced. That's the time to make decisions when the mind is in good shape. If you're in a low mood or not feeling okay, could I suggest that you don't make big decisions? Hold off until your mind is straight. Don't make big decisions under the influence of alcohol or anything else that makes you high. You're not seeing it straight. If you're on holiday and high on alcohol a street rep might try and push you into a taxi to take you down to the local timeshare development. If you've already had a few drinks, turn down the offer of free champagne.

Only make big decisions when you're okay, balanced and seeing things straight. The highs and lows of mood are bad for you in the decision-making process.

As an affirmation, 'I'm okay' is a good one. It keeps you grounded. You don't suffer the highs and lows. People tell me they love the highs (it makes them feel alive) and I understand that. The same people tell me that the lows can take weeks to overcome. They don't like the lows, although it's a good moment to remind yourself that you're okay still. Your mind will self-correct. Everything passes.

Could I suggest that you avoid negative affirmations? My former friend Dave bashed his subconscious with the affirmation, 'I am not depressed'. He had the habit of discussing his affirmation with lots of positive people and he couldn't understand why they didn't want to discuss it with him. It's always best to frame things positively like, 'I'm happy, I'm capable, I'm alive, I'm doing well, I'm okay'.

CASE STUDIES

Nicola's nightmare in Nicaragua

My student, Nicola, aged 23, is an amazing young lady. She now works for a charity. She's ambitious and takes on far too much responsibility. This often results in stressful situations.

In 2012, she travelled to Central America with her boyfriend for an extended period. While in Nicaragua both were abducted and taken to an empty house where they were bound and gagged for three days while the perpetrators cashed in on their credit cards. Under the cover of darkness, they were dumped in a car boot, driven out of town and left for dead by the side of the road.

They cried when the ordeal ended. A few miles down the road they stumbled across a small settlement. The locals provided them with food, water and shelter for the night.

"It was a horrendous ordeal," she said to the class. "One that I'll never forget. The aggression, the threats of violence, the waving of pistols was terrifying. I will never forget what happened nor will I be defined by what happened. I will not live in fear. I will live life on my terms. I will fulfil my potential. I am not afraid of anything."

It takes character to find that level of courage and then to express it so succinctly. To make this statement with such clarity and determination sent a shiver through the classroom.

We have all had our share of ups and downs. When we are deep into shocking negativity, it's good to know that we're only ever one thought away from the light.

Mark - The wheel of fortune

Imagine you're having a nightmare and the story goes like this: you find yourself in a London casino and you have a large suitcase full of £50 notes. You've sold your house, your car and you've cashed in your large investment portfolio. Your wife and children are concerned about your wild mood swings and why you've sent them away. The next stage of the plan is to play roulette and place all your chips on a number that you haven't yet decided upon. I am becoming tense just writing this because as high-risk plans go, it's one of the worst imaginable.

I tell you this because one of my students, Mark, told me his story. Thankfully, he didn't sell his house or car or send his family away. But he told me that his next speech to his directors and colleagues was of this level of importance. I didn't know the chap well but I imagined that he had a high-powered job. When I asked him about his work it didn't sound particularly exciting or high-powered. I was curious and asked him about the stakes in this game and what would happen if he succeeded with his speech?

So, the odds are 35-1 against and his answer was, "Nothing". Nothing would change if it all went well. And if the speech didn't go so well, he said he would lose everything. The word everything could suggest that he lost all his worldly possessions including the clothes he stands up in. The love and respect of his entire family, his company car and executive expense account. But 'everything' meant none of that. It turns out he might miss out on a promotion sometime next year, maybe, never.

This story is mental torture from start to finish. None of it stacks up. It sounds completely made up and it was, his overactive imagination and catastrophic visualisation. And yet if you're telling yourself this story day in day out, could you imagine how real it becomes when the subconscious mind can't tell the difference between reality and what you put in there? We create our lives (our reality) through our thoughts, moment to moment. If this story is running on a loop for any period of time it starts to look real. This whole story is in his head. I was so glad that we could identify the falsehood and then create a strategy based on real life events. What I found disturbing was his premise that his whole sense of personal security was wrapped up in a middle-management job role. And that without that job or the benefits it gave him, he could not function as a human being. That premise had to be challenged.

Ellie and boring work

Ellie is a young woman who works in bank administration. She's bright, funny and is incredibly articulate. She's popular in class and chatty with the other students. Her speeches are first class and she's hitting the highs I'm looking for. What is she doing on the course? I was intrigued. So, I asked her:

In a scathing tone she said that she disliked her job because it was making her miserable. The major issue was boredom. One of her junior colleagues had left the department and Ellie had inherited her 'low level' duties. One of these was fronting a security induction every Monday morning for new starters. The new starters come in mixed grades from director to bank clerks. She agreed to take this role on as a temporary measure. After three months she already felt like she was going through the motions. It had become so routine she described it similar to a pre-flight safety instructions display. Boring and repetitive - her words.

"How do you fake sincerity when you're so bored," she asked?

I suggested that she didn't fake anything. I reminded her that she had accepted the job. While she was paid for this work, it was her duty to instruct new colleagues to the best of her ability. Speaking is a leadership role. All these new recruits deserve a professional induction. Day one and she is the face of the company. It's important that she makes a good first impression. The new recruits are motivated and will absorb all that she says. She's in a powerful position to influence her new colleagues. This process takes thirty minutes per week. I suggested that this was the best job interview she never had. She has access to high placed individuals in the company. These individuals would become vice presidents and presidents of the bank. If she does a great job, she'll be remembered for the initial impact she had on them as a safe pair of hands. I asked her to turn things around and stop thinking about herself and start thinking more strategically. She had this golden opportunity to make herself known and network throughout the bank.

The challenge and desire of any speaker are to make your subject matter valuable and relevant. You have to find an interesting angle. I don't think the job sounded boring at all, just a change in attitude and application makes a huge impact.

Annie and charity

Annie is in her early fifties and she is a director of a London charity. Her background was as an economist where she worked in financial strategy. She chaired several conferences, seminars and events for diplomats, politicians and the judiciary. In recent years, her confidence has waned. She now works three days a week and feels excluded from some of the executive meetings that she once chaired and organised. She feels that her voice is no longer heard. She says that she's not as sharp as she was and that her colleagues don't think she's up to the job.

As usual in one of my 1-2-1 sessions, I asked her to prepare an ice-breaker speech which she did with aplomb. I call it an authenticity exercise. She spoke with great enthusiasm, conviction and sincerity for eight minutes. She was one of the best speakers I have ever worked with. It was clear to me that she had confidence, presence and a fantastic voice. Her thirty years' experience gave her incredible insights into the thought processes of the UK's top decision makers. I gave her my evaluation of her performance which went beyond the regular objective criteria for an ice-breaker. She was exceptional in every way. She urged me to give her some 'harsh' feedback, but I couldn't. I told her that she was a masterpiece. It would be unprofessional to offer inaccurate feedback. It would be like putting the Mona Lisa in a picture frame from a second hand shop. I wasn't prepared to do it. I played it back on the video and she started to cry.

For weeks she had been dreading our meeting. She had told herself that she was useless. She had told herself that that her colleagues were planning to make her redundant. She had told herself that her career was finished. When I pressed her on these issues, she told me there was no evidence. Just a recurring thought. These thoughts and feelings looked so real and created a paranoid view of her working relationships. Negative visualisation can be devastating.

Tony swimming against the tide

Tony is early middle-aged, works for an international bank and regularly pitches deals to clients and prospects. In the last two years he has made over ninety pitches and travelled around the world with his work on many occasions. The tide of work and expectation has taken over his life. His strike rate with his prospects is diminishing. He used to be confident when his conversion rate was high. Tony is a perfectionist and he's feeling the pain of not living up to his impossible expectations. Life and work are a slog and his personal relationships are suffering.

Tony has had suicidal thoughts, none of which he takes seriously. Though he's aware that suicide particularly in men of his age is at a frightening level. His one desire is to leave the corporate world and become a counsellor for men with serious personal issues.

In class, Tony demonstrates his professional qualities in exemplary fashion. He is fun and popular with the other students and supportive of his colleagues. He's an excellent speaker who demonstrates rhythm, fluency and he's highly articulate. Nobody believes him when he says that he lacks confidence because there's no evidence of it. Tony is torturing himself. He's telling himself stories that will look real to him, but nobody else.

A few months after the course, Tony contacted me. He had made the decision to go to night school to learn to become a counsellor and he is already volunteering with two charities for men. The corporate world had lost its gloss. Money, job titles and expense accounts mean nothing if you're unhappy. His mood has lifted, his family relationships have normalised and his mind has calmed. When the mental chatter ended, he found himself and a real purpose in life through the service of others. Now that he's managing his issues, he will be able to help others in a more congruent fashion. He's preparing a public speaking road show to help his target audience. It looks like public speaking wasn't his problem at all.

Spinning Jenny

Jenny is an NLP master. I know she's an NLP master because she managed to squeeze those words into three speeches in class. Jenny is a bright lady, quite a good speaker and confident in a social context.

Why on earth is an NLP master attending my course? Surely, NLP gives you all the tools and techniques to be an astonishing individual. She is after all an NLP master.

Jenny's mind is spinning because somebody has given her a title on a certificate that she neither understands nor embodies. I have nothing against NLP, quite the reverse as I have learnt so much from it. The big issue is that if you're in a field where your top priority is to help others, you must believe in what you're doing. The title NLP master means nothing to your client if you yourself do not show the confidence of your conviction and deliver the promise.

Public speaking isn't the real issue here. It's a symptom of beliefs and expectations which are not aligned. You'll never speak with conviction if you don't believe in what you're doing or if you're tripping over your job title.

Fleischmann and Pons déjà vu?

My student, Ivan, is a scientist. He's an amazing young man. He's bright-eyed, ambitious and has remarkable language skills. English is his third language which is so hard to believe. Ivan is tipped for great things.

There's only one thing creating an obstacle to Ivan's continuing success and that is the professor in charge of his research project. The professor has set a day for Ivan to present the team's research findings. Publish or perish is the motto in academia. It's all so exciting, isn't it? Ivan doesn't think so. Ivan believes that the research findings should be peer reviewed by similar teams in other faculties around Europe to substantiate the findings of their work.

Following the Fleischmann and Pons Cold Fusion debacle of 1989, common sense tells us not to conduct science by press conference.

Ivan is fronting his team's work and he wants it to be accepted only after external verification. If the research is wrong, incomplete or not bulletproof in any way, who is in the firing line? I am not surprised Ivan's feeling the tension because at this moment he is unsure of how well the project and findings will be received. His belief in scientific method is compromised by his professor's actions. Speaking, once again, isn't the issue here. It's the symptom of something more complex.

Josie's fields of sorrow

Josie is from Cambodia, she's extraordinarily petite and works for an international aid charity. She is one of the calmest, most charming and intellectual women I have ever worked with. We had a 1-2-1 session together and we started chatting about her past and her work ambitions. Her plan is to continue working in her role and eventually apply for a job at the United Nations where eventually she wants to become Secretary-General. Her only goal is world peace.

Then she told me the saddest story about her family. When she was five years old her father and three brothers went to work in the fields, as was their daily routine. They never came back. This was the late 1970s and the time of Pol Pot and the Khmer Rouge. The bodies of her family have never been found and there is no expectation that they ever will be. You can imagine the impact that this would have on the lives of her mother and young sisters whose world was turned upside down and had to learn to survive in a harsh, minimalistic agricultural landscape.

Despite that horrendous experience, there was not one ounce of bitterness or anger. There was, however, a steely resolve to this tiny woman's personality. She says she prays for her missing family every day. No amount of suffering will stop her changing the world in a powerful way.

Vince's last words (almost)

I have been in personal relationships which 'I believed' were wonderful and yet ended abruptly, painfully and disappointingly. I have had relationships which I ended for fear of increasing pain further down the line. Every bad experience, although not welcomed, opened a new door, a new perspective and a new opportunity. Other things and better things came along. Disappointments although painful provide the springboard for new and exciting life experiences. Had I not had all these experiences both good and bad, when my wife came along, perhaps I would not have been ready or available to welcome and accept her into my life. And where would I be now?

In my professional life I was once fired from a good job and I was also made redundant from a bad job. I have had jobs that I loved where the contract ended and jobs that I disliked where I was so relieved for it to finish. If you ever lost a job on the basis of one speech, I would suggest that it was the wrong job for you. As human beings we all need support and direction. If your job doesn't offer that support, there are millions of great jobs out there that do. Nothing can crush your spirit. It is unassailable. Your life is not dependent on your next speech whatever you tell yourself. Although you can convince yourself of anything.

PART 2

HOW DO I DELIVER

THIS?

THE THREE UNIVERSAL LAWS OF PUBLIC SPEAKING

If you put your finger on an electric hot plate, assuming it's switched on, you get burnt. It's going to be painful and you'll be more focused next time you're close by. The thing about hot plates is that they transfer heat, usually to pans or other cooking vessels. The hot plate doesn't care whether it heats a pan or burns your fingers. The law of thermodynamics holds no respect for its user base. It just does what it does. It's a universal law and as such it applies whenever one surface touches another or when heat is passed through air, water or gas. It's the same in public speaking. There are three principles that never change. An awareness, understanding and application of these principles mean that you're less likely to get burnt.

140

Strong communication skills are the cornerstone of your personal and professional success. We live and work in a knowledge-based global economy. Sharing ideas and concepts with our colleagues, customers and clients is top priority. How we communicate is essential. Remember there are two distinct aspects of communication; the message you transmit and the message that is received. Have you ever miscommunicated a message? Do you feel that somebody has given you the wrong impression or confused the message? It happens a lot. There are three key laws for speaking in public:

a) It's not what you say - it's the way that you say it.

This includes your word selection, your vocal variety and your body language. The voice is an expressive tool. The beauty of the spoken opportunity is to share with your audience your beliefs, thoughts, and actions around your particular subject. It's your opportunity to sell the message and allow people to buy into you as well as the material content. Mumbling, speaking into your notes and talking to the floor or ceiling will only frustrate the audience. Don't do it. I have tried and failed many times. Look the audience in the eye, smile and talk to them with respect, humility and empathy. Your role is to deliver a message with value. In fact, it's your only role.

Be alert, be alive and be real. Give it 100%. Bring your personality, creativity and spontaneity into your speaking. Give it your best shot. Even if it isn't great most people will warm to your efforts if they perceive that you're stretching yourself. Remember, they're not looking for perfection or encyclopaedic knowledge. They want to feel that the time invested in your speech will derive benefits further down the track.

b) Know your audience, their expectations and speak with purpose.

Everything you say must be themed and relevant to the audience's needs. Stay focused and remain disciplined. Every word is for the audience's benefit - not yours. You're the delivery mechanism and the conduit through which the message passes. You may feel that the spotlight is on you, but this is where you turn the spotlight back on to the audience.

Your audience will have an expectation. If the promise is one hour on how to save £10,000 in their business every year, focus on that issue. If you talk for ten minutes about your hobbies of stamp collecting and model railways, you're heading full steam down the track of disappointment. Stay on the promised theme and be clear about your purpose. What are you trying to achieve in this spoken opportunity? If you don't have a goal, I can guarantee it will be a victory for ramblers. People are busy these days. They are time-poor. If you waste their time, they are unforgiving because they know (and so do you) that that time is lost forever. Be remembered for positive and thought-provoking reasons.

There are seven speaking purposes to observe when preparing a speech:

to inform, to educate, to train, to persuade, to motivate, to inspire, to entertain

Discuss the purpose for the speech with the organisers and what they would like you to deliver and stay on that theme. If you try to tick all the boxes, you'll be jumping off at tangents and then it's hard to track back to your central theme. Even worse, you'll confuse the audience and lose them.

c) Plan, prepare and practice.

We are all familiar with the mantra of 'Education, education, education'. In public speaking, the mantra is 'Planning, preparation, and practice'. Why people try to 'wing' speeches is a constant mystery. The best way to create anxiety when you least need it is to avoid planning, preparation and practice. You have a date, a time and a venue and it's fixed. Praying for it to be cancelled is not a credible strategy. If you are a professional pianist and you don't practice several hours each day, it is unlikely you will be a professional pianist for long.

The dangers of procrastination

In 1984 when I died on stage in front of the Board of the Co-operative Wholesale Society in Manchester, the entire experience could be traced back to a lack of planning. Fail to plan, plan to fail – another victim of one of business' most treasured aphorisms.

When I received the invitation, I was only in position six weeks. I opened the brown envelope and I read the content at least twenty times. The Board would like me to speak to them in three weeks' time. The invitation was vague. They wanted me to talk to them. The same questions continually arose in my mind; why followed by why me? I was still establishing myself in the company. I was busy with many projects and I was trying to enjoy the pleasure of my new role, colleagues and environment. Why me? This was the poison chalice.

In hindsight, a good strategy was to write back immediately and ask what they wanted me to speak about. Even now many years later, I was clear that my speech needed a purpose. What I didn't have was the courage to respond. I thought that if I asked them an obvious question like that, they might think I was being 'funny', stupid or lacked confidence. So, in the end I did nothing and I thought I would try to charm them if all else failed. Within moments of entering the room, I fell to pieces. My ability to articulate no more than a handful of sentences flopped. To this day I still don't know what they wanted from me. But I was told that the invitation was not the poison chalice I had assumed. Quite the opposite in fact. I was told that they had heard good things since my arrival and that they wanted to get to know me. In five tragic minutes, I destroyed my reputation and my future prospects.

So, how do you prepare? My simple answer is thoroughly. Imagine an iceberg and draw a line where the 11% is above the water line. Assume this 11% is the delivery and the 89% below the waterline is the planning, preparation and practice. Have a purpose for making the presentation - what do you want to achieve from this spoken opportunity? It should have structure and no more than three key points. How long are you speaking for? Who will be in the audience? Where is the venue and how will it affect your delivery? What are the key points you want the audience to take away and utilise?

I wish I could turn the clock back, but only in the context of knowing what I know now. Things would be different.

'An expert is a person who has made all the mistakes that can be made in a narrow field.' – Niels Bohr

My first stop was the bookshop where I found a few titles on the art of public speaking. There was *How to Win Friends and Influence People* by Dale Carnegie which was expensive and *How to Overcome Nervous Tension and Speak Well in Public* by Alfred Tack. The latter had pictures in black and white of businessmen and women striking strange poses of which Gladstone, Eden and Baden Powell would be proud. First published in 1913, this was a superb introduction to the elusive art of public speaking.

At work I became determined to increase my visibility. I started talking and interacting with colleagues, sharing information and work insights. Eye contact increased to establish trust even outside of public speaking. This book was full of revelations. I then began to stand up and talk to colleagues in meetings. A bit of bravado, eye contact and subject matter knowledge seemed to leave a pleasing impact except for my colleagues who preferred the old Vince. By stepping forward like this I was challenging the status quo. By becoming more visible, my more ambitious colleagues began to see me as a threat. Speaking up and speaking out was quite addictive. I am not suggesting that at this early stage in my speaking career, I was particularly good. I was just no longer afraid of failure. As human beings we tend to catastrophize about the outcomes of the unknown. With public speaking, everything that could go wrong went wrong in the Boardroom and yet I was still alive, still 'popular' and I wasn't going to lose my job. This was an awakening. Everything looked the same, but everything was different. I had more energy. I wanted to start learning again.

The awakening did not last long. The habit of dodging the column doesn't disappear overnight. As soon as I had found my new comfort zone, I put up the shutters even though I wanted to explore this hunger of personal development. It was clear that by making waves and becoming more visible, I was creating an undercurrent of antagonism. My renewed energy was a turn off. My epiphany was viewed in a negative manner. I had become the office bore. Poachers become gamekeepers. Smokers become non-smokers and want to assert their rights on behalf of the world. This gift of a lightning bolt of energy was wasted. People liked the previous version of Vince; the calm, passive and invisible form of Vince. The Vince who was happy to be seen and not heard.

Panic Attacks

My capitulation in front of the Board was a classic panic attack. As I had never experienced a panic attack before, it was a frightening moment. Imagine losing control of your body to a thumping heartbeat. Imagine an extreme dizziness with shaky knees and a sensation that you're about to collapse. Profuse sweating and gasping for air are terrifying. The most frightening thing was that I didn't know at the time exactly what was happening to me.

It didn't take long to work out that my fragile ego had been exposed to public scrutiny. It started with the thoughts that I wasn't good enough. My next thought was that I wasn't prepared enough. Hence, I didn't know enough to speak to the top brass. Only one of those statements was true though – I was not sufficiently prepared. This was a massive mistake and a huge learning lesson.

Panic attacks are triggered by negative thoughts. Thoughts where we feel exposed, helpless or hopeless. Thoughts where we feel trapped and can't control the outcomes. A lack of oxygen to the brain triggers the amygdala to perceive a threat, and within a fraction of a second your entire body is swimming in adrenaline with the resulting physiological consequences.

The best strategy with panic attacks is to avoid them. With regards to public speaking, this is achieved by meticulous preparation. Deep controlled breathing over a period of time increases relaxation through improved oxygen flow. There will be more on breathing later.

I haven't experienced a panic attack since the mid-1980s and I am not surprised by that. My attention is so focused on my mind and body's needs. By this I mean I want to be properly fuelled (I care about what I eat), properly relaxed and properly hydrated. Then I can focus on delivering to the needs of the audience. I just know that I'm looking forward to the event and I'll give it my 100%.

Finding your Vision

Finding your vision as a speaker isn't easy. But if you're not looking for the big picture it's unlikely that you'll find it. At team meetings across the globe people talk about the contents of spreadsheets. They tell us about what's in this column and what's in that column. That the yellow bar chart has 66% next to it and is confirmed as yellow 66%. This is dull. This is not speaking it is assisted reading.

There are many speaking tasks at work that do not require vision. So, to avoid wasting colleagues' time, when we're talking about less important material, keep it concise. I remember team briefings would drag on for hours because speakers were unprepared.

In one company we couldn't leave the meeting room until all the biscuits were eaten. Leaving biscuits on the table meant that the budget for biscuits could be withdrawn.

I remember once giving an update on the introduction of a faulty document scanner in the late '90s when they were the latest technology. When the scanner didn't work it would take almost half a day of my time. So, when I updated them on the scanner project, colleagues laughed. They thought it was hilarious that my indignant protestations should cause such inconvenience. I then told them that losing half a day's productivity resulted in me working excessive overtime to catch up. More hilarity from my colleagues. Just because people wear suits and earn large salaries doesn't mean that they're professionals. As I mentioned, poacher turned gamekeeper. I began to value my time, even if my colleagues didn't.

This miserable experience had a profound impact. I was determined not to waste my career on serving people and companies that lacked ambition. I saw a lot of people going through the motions. I knew the signs because I used to be one of them.

By this stage in the late '90s, I was more comfortable with speaking and often asked to do some high-profile speaking work which I enjoyed. One day I read that the training department were rolling out a new help desk support product. They were looking for volunteer trainers from a technical background. The project was inspiring because I had never done a speaking delivery as intense as this before. I would deliver training to ten people with PCs, for one hour followed by a one-hour break. I would speak for twenty hours per week on the same subject. At last, I was almost my own boss. It was just me and the students. What could go wrong?

As you can imagine, it didn't work out. There were technical problems in the training room. Power problems, resource problems, software problems. If it could go wrong it went wrong. Initially, we only had five out of ten students in class. This became a massive scheduling, reputation and project issue. Despite telling our project coordinators that the classroom had catastrophic problems, they were unable to reschedule the extra 50% of the students. So, on day one and two, I received forty students per day, of which I trained one half. As one of the messengers, I received a great deal of abuse as did one of my female colleagues who decided that the life of a volunteer trainer was not for her. She quit as did the project manager who went on sick leave, never to return. Corporate chaos!

'Everything happens in a blaze of light.' – WB Yeats

At first the classes were awkward. It didn't flow, the structure wasn't working and students were asking difficult questions. They weren't disruptive they just wanted to know what they wanted to know. So, I reorganised the flow of content and created a FAQ for my project colleagues. This simple proactive act helped me become the project sage. Colleagues came to me asking advice on how to handle the classroom difficulties. I loved the intensity of the work, the feedback sessions and the camaraderie of my new colleagues. I noticed too that once I got into the flow of my speech, I began connecting the dots; making insightful statements and speaking with conviction and passion. I didn't know where that energy was coming from. I recognised a sense of purpose growing to deliver this problem project. I had taken ownership of these problems and made it my business to resolve them. There was a huge rise in my sense of personal value and I appreciated this massive boost in confidence.

The project lasted months. I met, welcomed and worked with hundreds of colleagues, most of whom now smiled and said hello to me in the corridor. The end of the project resulted in dinner, awards and a huge celebration. During the project, I had found myself and my confidence. I understood the need for coherent structures. I understood the need to address major student concerns early and I had learnt some basic psychology. I had begun to explore my voice. Every day, I put my voice through the gears and had a wonderful time. I was so confident in the material. I was determined to make this experience a game changer. Delivering a learning experience to so many people was an exhilarating way to spend the day. Who thought that one could actually enjoy public speaking and corporate life?

My vision was to deliver great technical sessions. Bring clarity from confusion and improve my personal contribution by delivering value to others. An idea hatched. I wanted to become a fulltime trainer.

I started attending meetings and presentations at work to observe other speakers and identify what worked for some and not for others. I framed two important questions in my mind:

a) what type of speaker did I want to be?

b) how did I want my audience to perceive me?

This was the beginning of an insatiable process of learning and self-development. Though not without its problems, it was a voyage of immense and intense discovery.

Vulnerability – 'Pressure creates diamonds.' – Dr Ivan Joseph

As a speaker, it's fine to be vulnerable. It is not a character flaw. We are all vulnerable at one stage or another in our lives. I have witnessed successful people experience career slumps and it can take a while to regain confidence. Being visible and talking about your disappointments and failures sounds hard at first. Of course, we all like talking about success, but success is just a word. The journey and struggle for success are far more interesting than the destination. The journey chronicles life's ups and downs, twists and turns, moments of doubts and insights. Our development as human beings is not linear; it's a convoluted path of trial and error, hit and miss, joy and frustration. Vulnerability is an attractive quality as it reminds us of our own humanity and how we help and support each other through difficult times. Our children are vulnerable and we love and protect them. We must remember that we were children once ourselves and it was our friends and families who guided, supported and nurtured us.

MIND AND BODY INTEGRATION

When your father's sperm meets your mother's egg the beauty of human creation begins. Cells divide and in a short period of time you begin to develop what becomes your brain and spinal column. Within there, fibres grow - your nervous system. On the ends of nerve fibres tiny buds appear; your heart, liver and kidneys and other essential organs. Your brain is connected to every cell in your body via the central nervous system. Your mind and your body are totally connected. What affects one affects the other. An average human being has trillions of cells. Every one of those cells lives an individual life and needs nutrition and care. I will expand on this later when we look at breathing and nitric oxide.

How many muscles do you have? 600 to 800? My chiropractor tells me that there is just one. As you develop, all the muscle tissue spreads out across your skeleton. Your muscles are all made of the same material. You have shoulder muscles, calf and thigh muscles (and many others). These are just identifiers or categories of muscles. Have you ever had a sports injury (say a dead-leg) and had to continue playing with a limp? One muscle may be incapacitated so your other muscles try to compensate for it. How do they know? That's easy because they're all connected. Let me reiterate that your mind and body are totally integrated. I repeat that every cell is connected to the brain via the central nervous system. It means that the status of your body can change in a fraction of a second. Imagine being chased by a sabre-toothed tiger. Your muscles need to react and respond quickly and in integrated fashion. A signal from the brain triggers a physiological reaction and those muscle groups have to act as one to save your life. It's the same with sexual arousal. A stimulus followed by a physiological reaction. Different organs but the same principle.

Speaking is both a psychological and physiological discipline. You're doing both together. Your mind and body are a phenomenal pairing, indeed the winning combination. Observe Olympic gymnasts, skiers and Formula 1 drivers. They are exercising split second judgments based on visual stimuli. What they're doing is dangerous and perhaps it's a good thing that they don't deliver a simultaneous commentary. Yet, the mind and body are stretched to the limit. It's not surprising that elite athletes develop into excellent speakers once their sporting career ends. They apply the same meticulous strategies that helped them become exceptional athletes.

The human body is engineered for high performance. Although we have yet to master the planet and the universe, man has mastered his local environment. He has learnt to hunt and survive, to study, to think creatively, to collaborate and to thrive. Man can travel in outer space and man can hold his breath for twenty minutes under water (Stig Severinson – World champion freediver). In terms of difficulty, for most people public speaking should rank somewhere on the easier side of these two extremes. We can do it! Every one of us.

SQUARE BREATHING

Imagine for a moment that you're in a meeting at work and you're surrounded by colleagues and clients. Each person in the room has to stand up and deliver a short briefing on team or project progress. As the action comes closer and closer you start feeling the butterflies fluttering in your stomach. We call this situation 'creeping death syndrome'. As the conversation creeps around the table towards you, you become more and more anxious.

Here's what to do. Take a deep breath in through your nose and as you do so, count to five. Then hold your breath for five seconds. Hear yourself count 'One – Two – Three – Four - Five'. Then exhale for five seconds through the mouth silently. Listen for the counting and finally pause for five seconds. It's called square breathing. I have been using it for years and students find it both relaxing and effective. It takes you into a defined breathing pattern. You have to concentrate to make it work. As you concentrate and breathe, your mind swings away from your speech and helps calm the nerves. Your mind can only focus on one thing at a time. It's a great distraction and a constant reminder to take advantage of oxygen.

This simple technique derives one of the biggest payoffs in overcoming the anxiety of public speaking. Utilise it when you're not planning to speak and notice how effective it is when you must speak. The calmness you're looking for is just a few breaths away.

Breathing and Oxygen

We breathe about 25,000 to 30,000 times per day, so this is big business. Our breathing is part of the autonomic nervous system which means that you breathe even while you are asleep. Because we don't have to think about it, we call it unconscious breathing. When we breathe unconsciously, we utilise up to about 66% of our lung capacity. In this section, I want to talk about conscious breathing where we can access an extra 30% of lung capacity/oxygen.

Learning to breathe effectively is your number one tool in managing anxiety. If you don't breathe well, you'll never conquer your speaking demons. The problem is that most people find the breathing solution too simplistic. People are complex and so need complex solutions. Because it's simple, breathing as a founding solution is easily dismissed.

Let me reiterate this key message. Breathing is the key to managing anxiety and public speaking. We need to raise the oxygen levels. If there's no fuel in the car, you're not going anywhere. When you breathe consciously it has a profound impact. It helps you improve in all areas. This improvement is not a surprise. It is inevitable. The more you focus on the task of breathing, the greater the payback. The most extraordinary change in my performance was when I learned how to breathe consciously. In through the nose, hold it for five seconds and out slowly through the mouth. This process slows the heart rate down. Lay flat on your bed, arms and legs uncrossed, allow the blood to flow unencumbered. Hold the breath longer and then exhale through tightly pursed lips. I can now hold my breath for up to two minutes and it slows the heart rate down. I feel calm and in control and so will you.

As we breathe in through the nose, the air which contains about 20% oxygen gets into our lungs and is redistributed around the body via your blood vessels. Our brain requires oxygen as do our muscle groups. When oxygen flows freely around the body all your vital mechanisms are supported.

We know so much more about the human body because health and fitness are prominent modern issues. Man has created remarkable tools like FMRI scanners so we can observe the distribution of oxygen in the brain in real time. We know that when we breathe in deeply, our blood vessels dilate. This improves blood flow and creates a greater throughput of oxygen around brain and body. We can see which parts of the brain are stimulated through oxygen flow.

As a young footballer I was told to breathe in through the nose and exhale through the mouth. When I asked why, the best answer given was that 'it seems to work'. These days, the scientific proof is compelling.

THE VAGUS NERVE

The Vagus nerve is about one metre long and it's the longest nerve in the body. It gets its name from the word vagabond (a wanderer). It wanders through the neck, the heart and lungs, the diaphragm and down through your intestines and into your reproductive organs. There is a right and left Vagus nerve, though it's usually discussed in the singular.

The nervous system is divided into two halves. First is the fight or flight – the stress system (the sympathetic nervous system). The second is known as rest and digest (the parasympathetic nervous system).

The presence of adrenaline in the blood kick starts the sympathetic nervous system. Your muscles contract, the heart beats faster and your blood pressure can remain high over long periods. Chronic stress created by a build-up of cortisol can cause a lack of productivity, followed by absenteeism and a general sense of burn out. You are more susceptible to strokes and heart attacks. Though mild stress is normal, if you think stress is bad for your health, it can be a killer. Listen to your body and slow down.

Cortisol is a survival hormone. You have to fight the sabre-toothed tiger or run. (Best run actually). Yet, thought induced anxiety has the same physiological impact and symptoms. Social anxiety, pressure at work, anything that creates stress continues and accumulates resulting in digestive problems. It also damages the immune system because while your brain is occupied fighting on one front, nothing is happening on the other side to restore the balance of your cells and muscles. Your food isn't digested and nutrient levels are diminished. Over an extended period, you can become unhealthy.

Second is rest and digest - (the parasympathetic nervous system).

Serotonin (a neurotransmitter associated with happiness and wellbeing)

Dopamine (a neurotransmitter associated with reward motivated behaviour)

In life, we need a balance. You shouldn't be too stressed or too easy going either. But it's important to be challenged in our studies, careers and sporting activities. If you're never challenged, you'll never know the full extent of the pleasures of achievement and you'll never become resilient.

We tend to operate more on the stressed side because of the mental stimuli we receive - too many tasks and not enough time. We are always chasing our tail.

So, breathe slowly, hold your breath and exhale slowly, and you tap directly into the parasympathetic nervous system. It helps to lower the heart rate and help you stay focused. Feel the shift of your mind arriving in that more relaxed place.

'Don't be fooled by the simplicity of breathing. It's highly efficient. How could anything so simple be so beneficial? Just remember that the nose is for breathing and the mouth is for eating.' – Stig Severinson – World champion freediver.

Try 1-2 breathing, so inhale through the nose for five seconds and then exhale for ten seconds. The double exhale sends the signal to slow down the heart. Try and make the sound of a sigh as you exhale. Controlled exhalation is essential for this process. Also try to relax the jaw as we tend to hold a lot of emotional tension there. Breathing is a neurophysiological technique and it's the cornerstone of public speaking. If you're not breathing effectively, you'll never have the fuel or the poise required to hit the speaking heights you're looking for.

NITRIC OXIDE (NOT NITROUS OXIDE)

Nitric oxide is a naturally occurring molecule of gas in your body. Its significance in restoring a healthy balance in the cells is well documented. It 1992, nitric oxide was awarded the 'Molecule of the Year' award and in 1998, Furchgott, Ignarro and Murad won the Nobel Prize in Medicine and Physiology for discovering nitric oxide as a signalling molecule in the cardiovascular system.

How does it work?

The endothelium is the lining of the blood cells and it's the largest organ in the body (on average 60,000-100,000 miles long) and one cell thick. It's key for distributing blood and oxygen around your brain, tissues and organs. The major cause of cardiovascular disease is a build-up of plaques within artery walls. In a healthy artery the blood flow is smooth and free and that's how we want to keep it. If the artery is hardened by plaque, it's less flexible and less effective. Relaxation is essential for life generally as well as public speaking. It's so much easier to relax when your body is working for you rather than against you. Nitric oxide is liberated from the amino acid l-arginine which is encouraged by selective foods (see below), and stimulated by moderate exercise and breathing relaxation techniques. There's every reason to take advantage of its curative attributes:

Over 100,000 studies into nitric oxide tell us of its importance in cellular activities where it:

• Improves communication between brain cells
• Assists in gastric efficacy
• Regulates blood pressure by dilating arteries (allows greater relaxation)
• Assists the immune system to kill bacteria
• Reverses erectile dysfunction

- Reduces inflammation
- Improves sleep quality
- Increases your recognition of sense (i.e. smell)
- Increases endurance and strength (body builders/athletes love it)

Nitric oxide naturally accumulates in your nasal cavity as well as throughout the endothelium. When we breathe in and hold the breath this incredible gas is redistributed around your body through the cardiovascular system. It penetrates the central nervous system and delivers its healing powers to your body's thirty to fifty trillion cells. To access this incredible molecule, all you need to do is breathe in through the nose and hold it and let it do its work. Once you reach the age of forty, your body begins to produce less nitric oxide which is in line with the ageing process.

So, we need to access and make the most of what is produced via deep breathing and yoga exercises. Green leafed vegetables like spinach and kale help generate a healthy supply of nitric oxide as do meat (animal organs particularly), walnuts, beets, garlic, onion, cayenne pepper, dark chocolate, shrimps, oranges, pomegranates and cranberries (all in moderation).

For many years, yoga, meditation and the Eastern traditions were frowned upon as they lacked scientific verification. Since 1998, there is a massive volume of research into the benefits of nitric oxide. It is free to use. All you need is to make the choice and start to access the benefits. Everything about nitric oxide is a winner.

Sleep

I have a great many young students attend my classes. For me anybody under 50 years old is young although I don't feel particularly old in my 50s. My students arrive on Saturday mornings following a busy working week and they look tired. Being connected 24/7 365 is normal practice, but it doesn't look like it's helping their productivity. Some students use their mobile phones as their alarm clocks (so do I). Some students have their phones set to chime every time there is an update on email or social media and they feel compelled to check their apps and respond. Sleep is a healthier option. We need to sleep and we need to sleep for at least eight hours per night. That's eight hours of undisturbed sleep. If you have a big job with lots of staff and huge responsibilities, then it's your duty to sleep and so must your staff. If you have a family, we need to remember that we have a responsibility to them too. Have you ever had a night of disturbed sleep? How do you feel in the morning? Grumpy, cranky, uncommunicative? Burning the candle at both ends is great fun. Yet, as a trainer, I realised that the late nights and the parties would soon be consigned to the past. I could not and would not face a class of ten people knowing that I wasn't present. As a trainer, I am sometimes up at 5am, and I hit the highway at 5.45 aiming for a 9am class one hundred miles away. It was hard at first, but the most important word is 'No'. No, I can't attend that event - no I can't go to that party. By putting your needs first, you show dedication and preparation for your professional duties. There will always be times to party when you're not committed the following day.

If you work in a high-pressure job and you find public speaking an awkward bolt-on to your daily duties, a lack of sleep is the last thing you need. Sleep has direct impact on your mood, motivation and general performance. It's good for the brain, memory and cognition, and it's good for your personal and working relationships. Giving a presentation while exhausted is unhealthy for you and your reputation and it's a low-quality experience for the audience. Those who are tired look and sound tired. If you're tired and grumpy, you don't want to be in front of a class or the Board answering questions when you're in the wrong frame of mind. A good night's sleep and a planned regime is a great boost.

When I am working in London, I have a strict routine. I am in bed before 10.30 pm and my alarm rings at 6.50. I do 10 minutes of conscious breathing to start the day. I leave home at 7.50 and take the 8am train which allowing for delays and cancellations should see me in class for 9.30 am. Having that sacred ritual gives me a focus and a sense of certainty which is good for confidence. As a trainer, the worst thing is to arrive late for class leaving a large group of students waiting for you. Life can be stressful enough without succumbing to bad planning. Having a coherent regime means I get a good night's sleep knowing that I am aware of the constants and managing the variables the best I can (an old programmer's joke).

Exercise

Going to the gym is not everybody's idea of fun. Neither is it everybody's idea of exercise. I am not keen on the gym myself, although in the autumn and winter that's where you will find me six to seven hours a week. I have a set regime, a flexible contract with myself and family that I attend the gym for an hour on days where I do not have clients or classes.

For me, great exercise is a walk in the park taking in the fresh air and the greenery. In the spring and summer, we'll go for a country walk for a few hours and then the reward is a pub lunch. Fresh air, pretty landscapes and a reasonable walking pace is all that your body needs to feel refreshed and invigorated. Contact with nature is a great motivator. Exercise releases endorphins and inhibits pain. Runners/athletes/gym goers feel euphoric highs similar to other opioids, and dopamine the reward hormone also provides a temporary lift. Cortisol, the stress hormone is washed from your system. Exercise is the best thing for you.

If like me you spend most of your life in an air-conditioned office or a centrally heated flat, the wide-open spaces are calling you for a good reason. Before marriage, most summers I would go on a walking tour to the Lake District. In 1995 I spent six months hiking in South and Central America. I have never been happier than walking in beautiful landscapes not knowing what I'd find over the next hill.

Why is this important for speakers? I find walking inspiring. It invokes ideas and takes you out of home and office. Everything looks possible when you're in the middle of nowhere on a sunny day and all you can hear is a faint breeze or the gurgling of a stream. We experience clarity of thought and connection with the landscape. We recognise that it's the simplest pleasures in life that offers the greatest rewards.

For those who prefer the gym, why not try an extended session? Do your usual routine and then add a mix of stretching and breathing exercises. For those individuals who find sleeping hard, this one activity will have a huge impact on all aspects of your life. Don't forget to remain hydrated in the gym. Drink water between exercises and warm-up for each activity. If you haven't exercised for some years, have a consultation with your doctor.

Walks in the countryside are now consigned to weekends and bank holidays (which are always busy in the UK). So, how about a walk to the park at lunch time? Even in big city centres you'll find parks with lawns and benches. Take some time out of the office and breathe. Slow your heart rate down and relax. Looking after your health is the best investment in your future. Operating with a clear mind is invaluable. Speaking with clarity is precious.

Rewards

The best reward is the knowledge of a job well done. But who says if the job was well done or not? In the public speaking context, it is difficult to be objective about your performance. Listen to feedback and ask trusted family members or colleagues to comment on your speech practice. There are speakers who speak well and yet deliver nothing of value. There are those who love the sound of their own voice and take an hour to say what could be said in five minutes. For nervous and novice speakers who find the prospect of speaking terrifying, start out with a reward in mind.

Look upon each speech or presentation as a separate project. Once the project is delivered, give yourself a treat. It could be a trip to the cinema, download an album or take your partner out to dinner. Associate the project with the reward and focus on the delivery. In your mind, every day is a step closer to the reward, not just your speech. Soon after I was married, I took a freelance project in South Wales for six weeks. With all the travelling, those six weeks seemed like an eternity. The reward was to take my Brazilian wife home for a month to see her parents. It worked as a motivating factor.

Every time you speak is a great learning opportunity. You've prepared and practiced your material several times and then one day you're delivering and something incredible trips off your tongue. You've just had an insight. A hidden truth has emerged from the speech, taking you by surprise. That truth like a diamond has always been there just below the surface and you found it. Because you were present in that moment of delivery you connected with the material and your conviction, belief and sincerity. You have found yourself as a speaker because when you connect with the material the audience will connect with you. When you find yourself as a speaker that is your greatest reward and there's no going back.

'The undiscovered country from whose bourn, no traveller returns.' – William Shakespeare.

Voice care and hydration

If you speak a great deal in your work it is best to avoid hot drinks like tea and coffee. The best thing for your voice is room temperature water. Not cold, iced or fizzy water, room temperature water only. Avoid excessive amounts of alcohol in the evening if you are speaking the following day. Never indulge in alcohol when speaking. If you're delivering an after-dinner speech, slurring your words is unlikely to enhance your professional reputation. If you feel that you are losing your voice and there is a big event on the horizon, most people will go to their local pharmacy and buy a throat medication. Although this will give you a feeling of relief, it will in fact dry out the throat even further. To keep the mouth, throat and larynx lubricated there is nothing better than room temperature water. What about lemon and honey? No – just room temperature water.

Hydration is another factor to consider when working. If you are 2-3% dehydrated, it can affect your concentration and memory by up to 30%. The message is to drink room temperature water. Your body is about 75% water. Your brain cells are different from other cells in the body. When speaking, I have a bottle of water handy as well as a glass. Drinking from bottles does not look too professional. Whereas taking a moment to pause and fill a glass makes you look like you're in control. Speaking is a leadership position. Looking like you're in control scores well with any audience.

Brain cells need replenishing, so hydration has a profound impact on your speaking by helping to keep everything in running order. There are long-term benefits for health and wellbeing by drinking water. Your muscles need fluids to work well. Water also flushes toxins from your system and it's the build-up of toxins that contribute to fatigue. For many years I have started the day with a large glass of water. After a good night's sleep, we become dehydrated. An early morning boost of water creates what I call the 'clarity' effect, which is why I feel so energetic and alive in the mornings. Early morning water boosts your metabolism. When you hear your tummy rumbling it's because the water has awakened it. Hold off the urge for tea, coffee and fizzy drinks as long as you can. Water delivers the best outcomes for your body.

If you are involved with any aspect of teaching, training, speaking and performance, you must always look after your voice. Unfortunately, many people involved in the teaching profession end their careers early because their voices are worn-out from shouting.

As speakers, the simple rule is to never strain the voice. This involves considerable restraint and self-discipline. If you like attending live football, rugby or cricket matches, it means that you should not shout. Shouting will make your voice hoarse. As a professional speaker, speaking with a damaged voice will only create further damage. When you have damaged your voice, it must be rested and protected. Speak little and rest a lot. If your voice has not come back to normal within a few days, it would be best to seek the attention of a doctor.

From September onwards (in temperate climates like the UK), most professional actors are seen wearing neck scarfs. Even indoors, most actors wear a silk cravat to cover their Adam's apple. Every jobbing actor knows that if he or she loses their voice, then they won't be working and that means no income. As actors spend long periods between productions, the last thing they need is a sore throat. The acting profession do not believe in bad luck where the voice is concerned. You have either protected your voice or not. This is the moment the understudy has been praying for.

So, room temperature water is the best thing for your brain, your memory and throat. Water is such a fundamental attribute of everyday life it is easy to ignore. Can I suggest that you give this point an elevated priority?

I have a few final suggestions, the first of which is to cut down on dairy products on the day that you're speaking. Milk and cheese produce mucous and there's every danger that you could spray the first few rows of the audience. This is not recommended.

I am interested in health matters and I am a big fan of both garlic and onions for the positive impacts they have on thinning the blood. Yet, the smell of garlic is not everybody's favourite, especially when sweated out of the body. I remember going to my dentist many years ago and he was telling his dental assistant about dinner the previous evening. The garlic from his breath was so strong, I didn't need an anaesthetic for my filling. So, beware if you're working close to people following an innocent curry.

SPEAKING DELIVERY

Planned conversations

'The art is concealing the art.' – Sir Lawrence Olivier

A speech is a planned conversation. That's it, a planned conversation. How many conversations have you had in your life? This conversation must meet the audience's needs and expectations. The audience has one thought and that is to receive value. Why else would they give up their time? Time is people's most valuable asset. Don't waste it – they want value and substance. Whatever you're talking about, it must be relevant. If it's not relevant, there's a mismatch between what you're delivering and their needs. The message is simple. Stay on the agreed theme for the session. Tailor it as best you can for your audience.

Who is the audience? Without an audience we don't need a speaker. Who are the audience in terms of their age and demographic? Are they shaped by age, purpose or identity? If you're talking to a group of bankers about economics, would you use the same material if you were talking to a class of 16-year olds? The key is to make the subject relevant and compelling. People are driven by self-interest. If there's nothing in the speech for them, it is unlikely to be a memorable occasion. Make your material relevant and always leave them wanting more.

Plan, prepare and practice. If you fail to do this last item, you're in deep water. Most speeches and presentations fail because of a lack of investment in time. As soon as you have agreed to make the speech, start planning. Start your research and start gathering material. If you have a fifteen-minute speech, it's easy to gather two hours' worth of material. Once you have your outline material, start considering the overarching message that you want to deliver. That's your speech's conclusion. From there, work backwards and start cherry-picking the supporting evidence which leads to that conclusion. Exploring three themes for four minutes each is much better than touching on a myriad of issues. Once you have the final draft of your speech, read it out loud a few times. If you're stumbling over words or phrases then redraft it so that you find new words and phrases that flow smoothly.

Once you're happy that your speech says exactly what you want to say, now read it into a free voice recording app on a smartphone. You can listen to the recording any time you wish. My travelling time to work and back each day takes about two hours. I can hear that speech many times per day if I chose. The beauty of this audible method is that it sounds like you're having a persuasive conversation with yourself. You're familiarising yourself with the structure and flow of the material and you'll know this material inside out by the time you come to deliver it. If Churchill had had access to a modern phone app, I am certain he would have utilised it for all his speeches. He was meticulous in his practice.

Aristotle's Rhetoric (or persuasion)

Aristotle was a keen observer of the human condition. His work dating back 2300 years set the gold standard for thought up until the mid-17th-century when modern philosophers started to explore science, society, politics and philosophy in what we now describe as 'the enlightenment'. This had a massive impact on the world but not on day to day communication where Aristotle's observations on rhetoric are just as important today as ever. Here's what Aristotle wants us to consider:

a) Ethos

b) Logos

c) Pathos

Ethos refers to the speaker's character. Do you like this person? Do you trust this person? Just a few hundred years ago, if you had title, wealth, land and family reputation, almost without saying a word you would be well regarded for ethos. The world has moved on and that no longer applies (mostly). Indeed, many titled, wealthy and well-connected people of good family reputation have been sent to jail for criminal offenses. These days your CV and the car you drive could be influential factors in how your character is perceived. When it comes to speaking, it's important that you speak clearly. Make sure that you are well prepared. Make eye contact (you can never establish trust with another human being in the same proximity without eye contact) and make sure that your material and tone of voice is appropriate for the audience. Enthusiasm, sincerity, conviction and passion say much about your character and your energy. Listening to a speaker who lacks energy will fail to convince the audience of anything. It also helps to speak with respect, humility and empathy. It's how you make the audience feel.

Logos refers to logic or structure, and there's nothing worse than a speech without structure as it will ramble, and become disconnected. Aristotle talked about inductive and deductive logic and tried to systematize thought with his 'Square of Oppositions' which is still a remarkable piece of work to this day. A speech needs structure. It must flow from one stage to the next in a coherent fashion, illustrating your argument with stories, anecdotes, case studies and other visual and memorable language. Whatever you say, you must believe it and bring it alive through your voice and energy for the audience to absorb and reflect. There are many speeches on

YouTube and TED Talks where excellent speakers weave a persuasive tapestry with their stories. Visual language is compelling. When the audience can see what you're saying, it looks real, it's hard to refute and it's persuasive. That's where Aristotle broke away from Plato and Socrates because he was fascinated by persuasion and not truth. Truth comes a poor second. If you don't believe me, just follow modern political debate and fake news.

Pathos is about emotion and appealing to the identity and self-interest of the audience. As human beings we display the thin veneer of calm and professionalism and yet just under the surface we are a bubbling broth of emotions. Were you ever overlooked for promotion? Were you ever let down by a loved one? Has anybody ever said something untrue or unjust about you and broadcast it around the office? Despite appearances we are emotional beings. We tend to make purchasing decisions based on our wants and not on our needs. That's why I have seven laptops, two iPads and two Android tablets. These technology companies know how to push my emotional buttons. My position as a business professional, a trainer (formerly of IT programming and administration) tells me that I need the latest tools and I need to keep up with the market and the technical horizon. My business needs to be wired 24/7 each day of the year. This is all true, because I receive emails and calls from people all over the world at all times of the day and night. I don't respond between the hours of 10 pm and 6.30 am. Although I am a classroom trainer at heart, it is technology and the technological outlook that keeps a roof over my head. There were many years where I ignored the temptation not to invest in my education which was my future. I will not make that mistake again.

So, my emotions say that I will not risk my future by a lack of investment today. Our emotions play an overwhelming role in our lives. By appealing to those emotions, we can affect great change in the world, much more so than by logic alone. Humanitarian organisations market their work using images of desperate scenes from around the globe. They are telling a story (of a child, a village or a victim) and appealing to our emotions to donate.

Imagine asking your bank manager for a £100,000 investment in your business. You need a compelling story to explain why you need the money. You must explain what you propose to do with it, and how it will be repaid on time. If you don't appear trustworthy, if you do not have a compelling reason and supportive evidence for the investment, there will be no investment. If your credit record is poor or if you've made regular late payments, how are you scoring on the ethos front? Your reasons for requesting investment would have to be overwhelming. The bank manager's emotions are saying that on balance, you're not a safe bet.

How do you feel when you watch political debates on TV? How do you feel when you see a politician that you don't like or trust? Does it make you switch channel? Electoral engagement is low because of a lack of trust. The perception is that whoever you vote for will not deliver their promise. People feel disconnected because of this state of affairs. In 2009, the UK had the parliamentary expenses scandal. What were the implications of confidence and trust here? Many MPs resigned voluntarily and many were forced to resign. What about MPs who make the law and who break the law? They too have a short shelf life. When trust is gone, your opponents always have a stick to beat you with both at a local and national level. Apologies are fine when they are sincere, but trust and confidence in politicians remains low. What about MPs who sell their time, influence and position to lobby groups? The best procedure is to resign and allow your constituency to start from scratch. Competence will always play second fiddle to trust.

Purpose

The purpose of your speech can be categorised under the following items: to inform, to educate, to train, to persuade, to motivate, to inspire, to entertain. As you can see, there is something of a logical overlap around some of these categories. Identify what it is you want to achieve and stay on that selected theme. Otherwise you'll find that you go off at tangents. Once you're off the path, it's difficult for the inexperienced speaker to pull it back to the main theme. Focus on the purpose of your speech and do not introduce irrelevant subject matter. Padding the speech out with unnecessary material disappoints and antagonises the audience. This is certain to run contrary to your aim.

Key Messages

Make sure that your speech not only conveys solid messages, but that it says a lot about you too. The audience are interested in your personality, your character and your beliefs and values. There's a point in your speaker development when you become the message (so you, the message and all of your personal attributes become one and the same thing). Have no more than three key messages in your speech. As we will see, three is the magic number in speaking.

Use your professional experience and personal creativity in the preparation process. We are all different so celebrate your uniqueness. Nobody can do it like you.

Most speeches are easy to forget because they do not focus on what they want the audience to think, feel or do. Focus on your messages and watch the speech come alive...

'It is impossible to speak in such a way that cannot be misunderstood.' – Karl Popper

Say what you mean and mean what you say (and keep it simple)

When you speak, you must demonstrate and deliver at least one of the following: enthusiasm, sincerity, conviction, passion, belief. Enthusiasm is the baseline. If you're not enthusiastic about your subject matter, then don't expect the audience to get too excited. There are exceptions – don't be too enthusiastic about making people redundant, for example. Everything you say is context sensitive – so make sure you really understand the context. If you can add some belief, sincerity, conviction and passion, the audience will love it. Say what you mean and mean what you say. Otherwise, it's an empty experience for you and them. Keep your words as simple as possible. It's easy to stumble over longer words, so keep them short.

This is a propitious moment to advise speakers who use long words to make themselves sound more perspicacious must desist forthwith for fear of antagonising their audience.

Churchill spent hours choosing shorter words for his speeches. Thought-provoking is good if you have a real grasp of the audience's capabilities, though if you make your audience stretch too far with the language, they will eventually lose understanding and interest.

Something to consider – a lot of speech content is repurposed for the internet. Unless you have endless time and resources to add subtitles, I would follow Churchill's advice. That means that more people from around the world, non-native speakers of English would have the opportunity to listen, understand and enjoy your message.

The law of threes (tri-colons)

There is a magic number in speaking and the magic number is three. Only ever try to make three big points.

We have an introduction, a main body and a conclusion to a speech. In some speeches we have a structure of problem, solution, and a call to action. In storytelling we have Goldilocks and the three bears. In the nativity story we have the three wise men. Here are some famous literary threes:

The good, the bad and the ugly.

Beans, Means, Heinz.

I came, I saw, I conquered.

Friends, Romans, countrymen.

Faith, hope and charity.

The Holy Trinity.

We call the three a completion. Most people can remember three things without resorting to notes.

Interestingly, Churchill said, 'All I have to offer is blood, toil, sweat and tears'. This is a four and it's one too many. Toil is usually omitted from the list - it doesn't fit in.

At the end of this session, I want you to be able to speak with confidence, coherence and clarity. This three uses alliteration. The delivery of the three has a rhythm and momentum. People who speak persuasively speak with a rhythm, flow and coherence.

In 2003, George Bush during a joint media statement with Tony Blair said, "What Iraq needs now is peace, justice and security." I am sure that in 2003, Iraq needed several other things. Yet, the tri-colon of peace, justice and security stands out in my mind because of the way it was delivered.

Structure

Churchill said that if you want your audience to remember your messages, you have to tell them three times. 'You have to tell 'em what you're gonna tell 'em, then you tell 'em, and then you tell 'em what you told 'em.' Below is a simple speech structure.

Introduction - (Tell them what you're going to tell them). This is the introduction.

Three themes are good. Remember the structure of a newscast.

Headline 1,

Headline 2,

Headline 3

Main Body

(theme 1) – put the flesh on the bones for the three introductory items. This is the meat of the presentation where you raise and support the significant issues.

(theme 2) – you can use stories, anecdotes, case studies, research and statistical data,

(theme 3) – metaphors and quotations (and other rhetorical devices) to make your points punch home.

Try and link the three themes where you can. When they are focused or tied together, it comes across in a memorable and coherent way.

Conclusion - (Tell them what you've told them). Reiterate major issues, pull it all together and make the audience 100% certain of your overall messages.

Speech Openings

When you begin preparing your speech, start with your conclusion foremost in mind. That way you can tailor your content, arguments and material towards that conclusive ending.

It's vital that your speech gets off to a flying start. Studies show that people listen most to the beginnings and endings of speeches. Creating a compelling opening and a memorable conclusion means that you're likely to score well with the audience.

There are many speech opening opportunities. Here are my favourite seven for impact.

a) A rhetorical question - Did you know that three teenage children die on the roads of London every month? Always follow a rhetorical question with a long pause to allow the audience to absorb the point. You want them to passively participate on the theme.

b) A startling statistic - Only 25% of 25-year-olds have considered pension provision... Remember that statistics can convince us of almost anything depending on the way they are spun. Remember too that statistics are plucked from the air by the speakers. It's good practice to cite the sources of the information. It builds your credibility with the audience so use credible sources for your statistics.

c) A bold statement – By 2040, the UK will be the world's largest economy. This one statement would get you wondering what has happened to the US, Russia and China? You must now support that opening with compelling evidence.

d) Tell a story – People love stories. Our love affair with stories begins when our parents read to us as children. Stories are visual. We relate to stories because our lives run through concurrent threads. For example, I am a son, a brother, a father, an uncle, a great uncle, a godfather and that's just in the context of my family. Each role within

that domain contains a series of related and unrelated thr
speeches, we tell a story to make a point. The point of tł
stacks up the evidence in your favour. We cherry-pick our _._.כ,
anecdotes and case studies to substantiate our major premise. If you
start with a story, its ending and point must land on the doorstep of
the story's theme. If it does not, it will confuse the audience.

e) A quotation - 'All experience is subjective.' It's expected that you
tell the audience who made the comment, Gregory Bateson in this
case. Otherwise people might think that you are looking to take the
credit for the quotation. Only quote famous people (or people at least
that you can Google). Quoting your great uncle David on the virtues
of global warming may not get people to buy into the credibility of
your argument. Unless your uncle's surname is Attenborough.

f) Project a startling image that grabs your audience's attention. Give
the audience time to view the picture and 'see' the point. Don't spell
it out for them. Let them work it out for themselves.

Memorable conclusions

Most speeches neither need nor deserve a rousing 'Free at last, free at
last, thank God Almighty, we are free at last' ending. This line is
taken from Martin Luther King Jnr's, 'I Have a Dream' speech which
was voted the most influential speech of the 20th-century. But that is
not to say we should neglect the speech's conclusion. An optimistic,
upbeat ending sounds professional. It leaves your audience feeling
that they have invested their time wisely and that they have some new
options for the future.

At the end of a speech workshop, I thank the class for their hard
work. I praise them for their progress and I wish them every success
with their ongoing development. Of course, say it with sincerity. You

need to make eye contact and it must be given in an open and optimistic fashion. If you don't believe in your words or you're saying it because you see it as the last chore of an exhausting day, then don't bother doing it at all. If you don't believe in what you're saying, it will come through in your voice and your body language. You can only have personal impact if you are committed to your message.

Have you ever noticed that speeches delivered at party conferences always end with a call to action? Whether the party is in government or opposition, it is the leader's job to galvanise the party's activists to do ever more canvassing on the doorstep, persuade businesses and individuals to make donations, and to continually motivate and give incentive to the party faithful to continue with their support. If you are in government, there is always so much more to do, so many priorities and so little time and resources. In opposition, you have to discredit the government's plans, develop even better policies and then convince the electorate that you are fit to lead the country once again. It is necessary to win back their hearts, minds and votes.

David Steel at the Liberal Assembly in 1981 told his members 'to go back to your constituencies and prepare for government...' A clear call to action and one that is memorable for many reasons.

If your speech conclusion is downbeat, defeatist or depressing, you can expect a room full of empty seats at your next presentation.

Always aim to be optimistic and upbeat. Wherever you are in any project or strategy, no matter how many hills there are to climb, as an individual voice you have the opportunity to motivate and energise your audience. Every speech has a context. If you had to make a speech telling staff that they are to be made redundant, I would suggest that your tone and body language reflected the seriousness of the situation. Always think through the context and ask yourself, what would be the best outcome?

Gestures

Eye contact is the most important aspect of body language. If you have great substance and value in your material, the audience will forgive you any technical idiosyncrasies. That said, no matter how well you know your subject matter, a lack of eye contact will destroy the impact of your speech.

Our gestures and facial expressions account for a large percentage of this impact. If for example the speaker is smiling before and during the speech, it sends a message of confidence. Note the impact of a speaker who does not look like they're enjoying themselves, it could send a message of stress or discomfort. If you're delivering bad news and you are wearing an inane smile, this will not deliver the results you're looking for either. If you're discussing sensitive material, your facial expression, voice tone and word selection have significant impact.

The bigger the auditorium, potentially the larger the number of people. Therefore, it's important to make your gestures larger as people at the back of the room need to see what you're doing too.

Vocal variety

In public speaking we talk about the 4ps. Pace, pitch, pause and projection. Vary the pace and pitch. If you utilise the same speech pattern, your voice will come out flat. If you speak rapidly you diminish opportunities for the highs and lows of tonal variety. Pause for two or three seconds after making a point. That time may seem like forever to you, but for the audience it just gives them a moment to absorb your last point. With a big audience increase your volume. Yet be aware that talking at full tilt is tiring. If you're not used to extended projection, there is a tendency for your voice to tail off towards the end of sentences. Try to avoid negative patterns.

Visual Language

Most people have a strong visual channel for learning. They say that a picture paints a thousand words and knowing this is helpful in putting across our messages to the audience.

Why do people squirm when they see a PowerPoint presentation covered in bullet points and small print fonts? It's because the brain handles images so much better than words. You want your audience to 'see' the meaning.

As children, we love stories. They fuel our imagination. They take us from our humdrum world and deliver us to a universe of possibility. As adults, we continue our love of stories through novels and films.

Open any page of your favourite novel and you'll see that the author is filling your mind with images. Some of the text is descriptive and some uses suggestion where it invites you, the reader, to fill in the blanks. Have you ever seen the film of a book and not liked it? When we read a novel, we create the characters and the landscape. Our mind works in pictures not words. When a film director creates that book in their mind's eye, it is their subjective interpretation of the text.

As speakers, we should use colourful and descriptive language where appropriate. But if you use too many adjectives or too much hyperbole, the whole narrative becomes cluttered. Both speaking and listening should be a pleasure. Keep the language simple and accessible and try to build a momentum.

By encapsulating your key messages in the form of stories, anecdotes or case studies you guide your audience to arrive at your conclusion. When they can see the evidence with their own eyes, that evidence is hard to ignore.

Use of Notes

Notes can either make or break your speech. It's vital that you cover the material intended so prepare notes to detail your structure and content (unless you know your content inside-out).

If you write notes in a script format there is the danger that you might read from them. In doing so, you disconnect from the audience due to a lack of eye contact. If the audience thinks that you are reading your notes, it will be less convincing. The spoken opportunity is designed to provide expression. Don't stifle your connection with the audience.

There are lots of different methods for notes; bullet points, mind maps, 6 x 4 inch cards and you can use PowerPoint for the structure of your speech. A lot depends on your speech purpose and its duration. All these methods are effective so long as you are confident with your material. I have tried to use PowerPoint to help prompt me but I find that it stilts my delivery. It doesn't flow the way I want it to. PowerPoint demands an order of delivery. My preference is to respond to my audience's questions in a more spontaneous fashion.

The best thing is to try them out and find which one works best for you. Here are three considerations for an effective speech: stay on track, speak to time and always be generous with your eye contact.

Humour

Humour is an advanced technique and you should give the matter careful consideration. If you find the adoption of humour easy, it's a great tool to have in your tool bag. If you find it challenging, then perhaps err on the side of caution and omit it.

People often ask if they should start with a joke, getting an early laugh or smile and breaking the ice. If you're confident and can deliver a joke it can create positive momentum. But make sure that the theme of your joke is on the same theme as your speech. If the joke flops for whatever reason, it can knock your confidence and hold you back.

Old and contrived jokes are best left out. You will score best by using your observational powers. Comment on something topical that is relevant to your theme or allude to something that has happened at the event.

The best humour is where we reveal a few of our personal fears, foibles and failings. We are all works in progress and whatever our subject matter, we were all once beginners and made our share of mistakes. Humility is an excellent way to connect with the audience. Tell them a funny story about what went wrong. You will connect with your audience at an empathetic level. You will be perceived as more honest and credible. If you are seen as over-confident, overbearing or arrogant, it doesn't matter how well you know your material or how much experience you have in your field, you have created a divide between you and the audience. Self-deprecation works well. It means that you can have a laugh at yourself and you can steer people away from the pitfalls. A strong sense of humour is the best protection against the most hostile audience. If the audience can see that you're relaxed and comfortable with yourself, they'll laugh along with you. If you take yourself too seriously, you'll need a suit of armour for protection.

Building rapport

Rapport is what happens when there's nothing between you and your audience. You are free to be you. Don't hold back on who you are and what you can offer them. Ignore the voice in your head. Ignore all the doubts and speak your truth. That's one definition of rapport. If you have any toxic goals clouding your thinking, it's going to trip you up. Below is a more technical definition.

How do you establish rapport with your audience? My simple equation for this is: respect, humility and empathy. If you speak to any audience with these three attributes, I am certain you will receive a warm reception. Use your personality, your facial expressions, your smile, and your eye contact. Make sure that everybody feels that you're talking to them individually. Respect your audience, empathise with them and recognise where they're at (personally, in business, in their world, depending on the context), use appropriate humour and sincerity.

Proximity - get close to the audience without invading their personal space. Your body language must be open and congruent with what you're saying and the way you're saying it. Be spontaneous and in the moment - feel your speech. Get them to engage by asking rhetorical questions. Voice tone - the warmth of your voice is so important and must be appropriate for the message delivered. Respect, humility and empathy are the most valuable assets of any speaker to connect with any audience.

Avoid Distractions

'The strength of a man's virtue should not be measured by his special exertions, but by his habitual acts.' – Blaise Pascal

There are so many ways in which we can distract our audience. The list below is not exhaustive:

Avoid rocking and swaying. It's hypnotic and gives your audience permission to zone-out. Firmly plant your feet under your shoulders and stand up straight. Put your body weight on top of your pelvis. Eye contact comes from the hips. Don't be afraid of moving and if there's space always move with purpose. Do not prowl around the stage. Involuntary movement is a massive distraction.

Verbal mannerisms: So, ok, y'know, right, init, blindin', etc etc., is that ok? yeah? do you get it? Bla bla bla...

Avoid ums and ahhs. Replace them with natural pauses.

Gentlemen, keep hands out of pockets especially, if there are coins or keys. The jangling effect distracts. Avoid scratching your head, chest, nose and ears. Generally, it's best not to scratch at all as it's not attractive viewing. Ideally, keep your hands away from your hair. If it looks like preening, the audience could get the impression that you're vain. As we've discussed, perception and reality are two different things, and the significant question is, how do you want them to perceive you? If you have long hair tie or clip it back for the duration of the speech. You can always let your hair down later.

Glasses - either keep them on or take them off. As we get older our eyesight deteriorates. Contact lenses or good bifocal glasses can save the day.

Communication Zone - We call from the top of the head to the navel the communication zone. Keep your hands away from your face – don't obscure your mouth. Anybody hard of hearing and using lip-reading will drop what you said and they could feel excluded from the conversation.

Avoid clichés like the plague - I have been told a million times about using this one...

Avoid jargon and acronyms with lay audiences unless you tell them in advance by means of a glossary of terms.

If you find yourself mid-speech creating a distraction, stop doing it. Don't mention it and there's no need to apologise. Carry on. The audience are not interested in your recent past. Make this moment and the rest of your speech memorable, right now, each moment as you deliver it.

VOCAL EXERCISES

You and your voice

The human voice is the most expressive communication tool. It is just as distinctive as your signature or your fingerprints. The moment you say "hello" in a telephone conversation, a good friend or family member will recognise your voice immediately. This uniqueness is something that developing speakers must embrace. There is no limit on the number of excellent speakers that the world can produce. It's worth examining the qualities and attributes of your voice to make it more pleasing for the audience.

Some people are born with a marvellous and memorable voice. They can even make the most of it. Many individuals need some help to make it sound more energetic or vibrant. The development journey is a fun and exciting experience. But it's different for everybody. There are so many paths to a new and improved voice. You could quickly become addicted to this form of development.

There are many facets of an effective voice. This section looks to touch on the myriad of opportunities available to the developing speaker. A balanced and concerted effort of ten to fifteen minutes per day over a period of six weeks usually sees significant improvement. It is unrealistic to expect changes to the voice overnight. Remember that if your voice has followed the same pattern over a period of thirty years or so, it is not only your vocal patterns that must be changed, but also your neurological patterns. Beware that if practice is not sustained, it is natural that your voice will slip back into its familiar and comfortable patterns of behaviour.

Everyone's voices are different even though we all effectively have a similar apparatus. Listen to your voice, as if you had never heard it before. What do you think about it?

Imagine that you are listening to a speech in your living room with the light off. You cannot see the speaker - you just hear the sound of his voice. Or not even that - imagine that you are listening to a female journalist talking on the radio. All you have is the sound to keep you awake, to give you information, to surprise and inspire you. That is the subject of this section.

The instrument is the voice...

The content in this section covers:

- Firstly, how you can improve your voice
- Secondly, how you can use it effectively
- Finally, some related issues and many exercises to practice.

THE FOUR PS

In public speaking, traditionally we talk about the four Ps. The four Ps are pace, pitch, pause and projection.

Look at the following recording files and observe the speaker when he talks at the same pitch and pace. If we consider the voice to be a wave of sound, the voice that always speaks at the same pitch and pace inevitably becomes flat or monotone (take 1). The voice flattens out because the wave is mostly constant. There are no highs and lows. There is little vocal variety. The wave is operating through a narrow spectrum of sound. It is our vocal energy that keeps your audience on the edge of their seats.

Look at the second recording (take 2) and see the same words. Look at the two voice files below and see the difference of the sound wave.

The wave file below is the recording from take 1 which shows a flat voice with little variation.

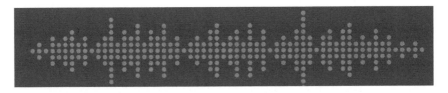

In take 2 we can see the highs and lows of tonal variety.

The speaker must always work the voice, changing the pitch and pace to make the voice interesting for the audience. If the speaker becomes excited about a particular issue, it is normal for the voice to rise in volume (projection) and be delivered more quickly than usual (so a change in pace). There are many vocal development exercises to assist your projection throughout this section.

Similarly, a speaker addressing serious issues in a speech should slow down, stretch out the pauses, and give the audience more time to absorb the messages. In Churchill's, 'Blood, toil, sweat and tears' speech, notice the slow pace and laboured voice. Note how the voice reflects the sombre mood of the situation. Note the strength of the pauses. The pauses build the drama in what was one of the 20th-century's biggest moments. Sometimes, his voice is little more than a whisper, but the weight and clarity of the words and their significance convey a powerful message.

Generally, the pause should last for two to three seconds, which for many speakers seems like a long time. But for the audience it gives them a moment to catch up with you. The pause is the speaker's best friend. During the pause, there is a moment to breathe and change eye contact before continuing the speech. Think of it as a mantra and watch your effectiveness as a speaker grow. The mantra is: 'Pause – breathe - change eye contact.'

BREATHING AND RELAXATION EXERCISES

Before indulging in any form of physical exercise, please ensure that you're fit, flexible and healthy. Always consult a doctor if you have any doubts or concerns about your health. If you feel uncomfortable at any stage during these exercises, please refer to the appropriate video and ensure that you're doing the exercise correctly. If you have any other physical concerns you should consult your physician.

https://player.vimeo.com/video/155313874

Introduction to Health & Safety regarding Public Speaking Exercises

https://player.vimeo.com/video/155315176

Why do posture, breathing and relaxation exercises?

ANATOMY AND PHYSIOLOGY OF THE UPPER BODY

Let's start with the body's four resonators which are the nasal cavity, the mouth, the throat, and the chest. Effectively, these resonators produce your voice and all four need to be free and uninhibited. Put two fingers across the bridge of the nose and squeeze. Now say a few words. You have just changed your vocal dynamic as well as the natural behaviour of the four resonators and I'm sure that you can hear that the resulting sound is less than pleasing.

Breathing – diaphragmatic breathing - The diaphragm is at the bottom end of the lungs and has a large storage space for breath which is often unused by speakers. Stand up straight and breathe in deeply through the nose until your abdomen feels comfortably full. Hold the breath for 4 to 5 seconds and exhale slowly through the mouth. Repeat this exercise for two minutes. Deep breathing provides two key benefits to the speaker. Firstly, if you feel nervous or apprehensive, the deep breathing will slow everything down. We want to establish rhythmic and smooth breathing. Oxygen floods the brain and makes you feel calmer. When calm and rational we make better decisions. As a speaker, it's imperative that you stay in control of yourself, your body language and your key messages. Secondly, the quality of a speaker's voice is determined by good quality breath control. Imagine the voice as a wave of sound. When the wave is well formed and sustained by quality breath control, it will be a more pleasant experience for you and the audience.

The four resonators

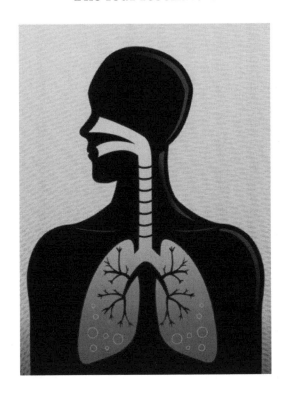

THE THREE HEAD RESONATORS

Now examine the width of your chest in comparison to the width of the throat, the mouth and the nasal cavity. The chest is wider and more voluminous than the head resonators. To produce a strong and vibrant voice, it must resonate throughout the chest. Think of an acoustic guitar – you stroke the strings, but where does the tone of the guitar resonate? Its resonant tones emanate from within the box. The chest is our top resonator - this is where the boom or vocal energy is generated. A point worth considering is that an acoustic guitar's shape is constant whereas the diaphragm is incredibly variable. Violins are small and narrow and produce a high pitch frequency. A double bass is at the other end of the sound spectrum with a big frame and low pitch frequency.

Breathing – diaphragmatic breathing. The diaphragm is the dome or parachute shaped muscle at the bottom end of the lungs and has a large storage space for breath. In everyday conversation, the diaphragm remains passive. As a speaker, to produce sustained vocal energy and vigour in the voice, the diaphragm must be engaged. The lungs are the engine room of the voice.

Trachea, rib cage and lungs

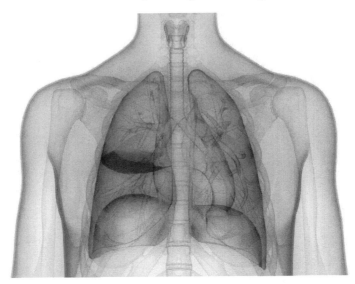

Trachea, lungs and diaphragm

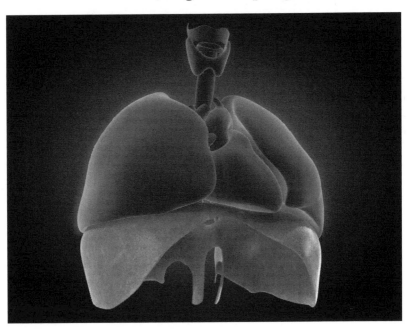

Enclosed are a selection of 40+ videos on the subject of public speaking and vocal development. There are breathing exercises, advice on posture, anatomy and physiology and vocal development. By exploring these exercises, you'll find a new sense of centred calmness. By working the voice and enjoying the new freedom found in your vocal delivery, you can go on to become a confident and dynamic speaker. You'll see that I'm having a lot of fun with these exercises and explanations. My first attempts at public speaking were not good at all. These exercises over the years have given me the confidence and wherewithal to speak to audiences around the world, without tension or inhibition. The battle for the emerging speaker is to stand at the front and be your best authentic self. When you achieve that, then you can relax for a while or at least until you start preparing for your next speech.

You'll find more detailed explanations for some of the videos further down the chapter. As you'll be working through the videos multiple times you'll know which text works for which video.

The videos are short, usually 1.0 minute to 3.0 minutes. Please take the exercises seriously, they each make a significant point. But during the exploration, don't take yourself or the sounds you create too seriously. A lot of people give up too soon because they expect great outcomes on day one. This exploration is a continuous development. I have been working on my voice for over 20 years. I find it pleasing, enjoyable and it's a beautiful and rewarding escape from everyday life.

The videos are small bite-sized chunks of useful information. It's best if you practice the exercise straight after the video ends.

The three head resonators (nasal cavity, mouth and throat) and the lungs/diaphragm

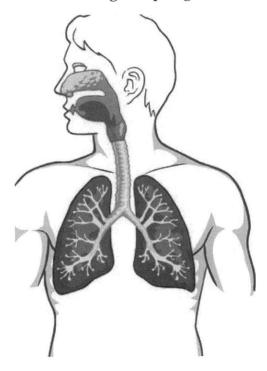

If you can breathe life and fire into Shakespeare's words, there is no reason why you cannot do it with your words.

Let's now examine takes 5 and 6. In take 5, the speaker once again is going through the motions. He is doing what he is doing, but he looks and sounds like he wishes he were somewhere else. In take 6, look and listen to the rise and fall in the voice. Feel the warmth, colour and interest in it. Note the emphasis on some words and not on others. Sometimes we need only emphasise the first syllable of a word, or the last, or even a syllable in the middle. Notice how he is trying to bring the story alive. The secret is vocal energy and that secret resides within us all.

And finally, in this section, let's come back to the pause. I repeat that the pause is the speaker's best friend. Pause, breathe and change eye contact. In Barack Obama's 'Berlin' speech, watch for the pauses and observe how the pauses create a sense of anticipation. Here is a man who can look out to a worldwide audience, smile, and not feel obliged to say anything. This gives him a remarkable aura of authority. He knows that he is delivering something of value and he knows that his audience will wait for him. Had he rushed those moments, it would have diminished the impact.

 https://player.vimeo.com/video/152139303

The power of the pause

 https://player.vimeo.com/video/155315176

Why do posture, breathing and relaxation exercises? The purpose of vocal development is to increase your vocal confidence and your ability to move an audience. Most people only use a small fraction of their voice's potential. By doing development exercises regularly, you will find your true potential and discover where it can take you.

 https://player.vimeo.com/video/152139311

Warm-up exercises – we start with some gentle swaying to warm-up the upper body muscle groups and activate the vocal apparatus. Think of your voice as a muscle. If you're going to do anything potentially strenuous, it's wise to start gently and warm-up those muscles. A friend of mine lives 200 metres from a motorway junction. He has to drive his car for a few miles first before he joins the motorway, so that he doesn't damage the car.

 https://player.vimeo.com/video/152139302

The three head resonators and the lungs – you have your mouth, throat and nasal cavity as head resonators. The lungs are the engine room of the voice. Your voice is a wave of sound and each of those entities contribute to the quality of your voice. There's a demonstration of what you can consciously do to bring more life, energy and dynamic to your voice.

 https://player.vimeo.com/video/152139303

The power of the pause and why it's so important. The only time you can breathe when you're speaking is when you pause. If you don't pause, that suggests you're talking too quickly – not so much speaking, but gabbling. The technique here is to always have enough energy in your lungs to deliver the line effectively. The pause delineates the words and gives the audience a moment to process what you've said. The pause also creates drama when required.

 https://player.vimeo.com/video/152139306

The diaphragm acts as the lower end of the lungs. So, when we take a really deep breath, we create this massive resonating chamber which I describe as the engine room of the voice. The head resonators are small by comparison and create more higher pitched frequencies. The boom and energy in the voice comes from the diaphragm and the chest.

https://player.vimeo.com/video/152139305

We discuss muscle tension in the upper body and where it comes from. Your body tries to create a harmonious balance. Overwork of one muscle group creates tension. Simple every day activities like carrying a briefcase or rucksack creates tension. Similarly, if you're on a long-distance car journey, every time you stop the car, you get out and stretch your muscles and get the blood flowing. If you think about all of the organs in the ribcage, they have been compressed by your sitting posture in the car. So, when we stretch, the organs will settle back into their default and optimum positions, giving you a feeling of relief and comfort.

 https://player.vimeo.com/video/152148153

Conscious and unconscious breathing - generally when we breathe, we're breathing unconsciously. That means we're only ever using 66% of our lung capacity. When we breathe consciously (more deliberately and deeply) we can increase that by 20-30%. That has a profound impact on the intake of your mind and body's fuel – oxygen. It's oxygen that makes us feel calm and in control. If you can master your breathing, you can master public speaking. This a foundation upon which you can build your speaking improvement. Never underestimate the power of the breath.

 https://player.vimeo.com/video/152139307

Posture, breathing and relaxation are at the heart of good speaking. The more relaxed you are, the more confident the delivery. But it all starts with great posture. Standing up straight allows your physiology to work at optimum efficiency. Actors talk about feeling grounded and it is a strong metaphor. Feeling that connection with the floor supports the dynamics of your upper body. Think of a high-rise building. It needs strong foundations. When the structure is solid you can start thinking about the furnishings. If a building's structure isn't solid, it doesn't matter what you do with it. It will always be wonky. You wouldn't want a reputation as a wonky speaker.

 https://player.vimeo.com/video/152139309

Breathing exercises – here we work through a small number of conscious breathing exercises to stimulate the parasympathetic nervous system, oxygenate the body and calm the heart down. If you're going on either a long or short car journey, it's worthwhile looking at the fuel gauge first. If you haven't got the capacity in the tank, you need to top up. When we breathe deeply, we're topping up the tank. We also activate the parasympathetic NS, commonly known as 'rest and digest' as opposed to its more commonly known opposite, 'fight or flight'. Activating the parasympathetic NS also sends signals to other organs that all is fine in your anatomy and physiology.

 https://player.vimeo.com/video/152139312

Neck exercises – your neck is one of the busiest parts of the body. It contains your windpipe (trachea), your oesophagus, your spinal column and, of course, your neck muscles. Your neck is narrow compared to the upper body. If you're suffering neck, shoulder or back pain, public speaking is probably uncomfortable for you. So, the secret is to remove the tension from the neck with some gentle exercises.

https://player.vimeo.com/video/152139310

Neck 180 & 360 degree exercises – it's important that we have a full range of movement in the neck muscles. These two exercises should be done slowly and with caution. We're always looking to tease out tension from the neck.

 https://player.vimeo.com/video/152638776

Jaw exercises – it's not unusual for people to hold a lot of tension in the jaw. We need to move the jaw up and down as we articulate words and sounds through lip movement. If you speak without moving the jaw, words will become indistinct. It's called frozen jaw. The purpose of communication is to convey a coherent message. If the message is not conveyed then communication did not take place. By warming up the jaw, it helps lip movement and improves the articulation of the word's syllables.

 https://player.vimeo.com/video/152638777

Stretching exercises – this exercise is excellent for accessing a full body of oxygen. Your muscles contract and relax as the large intake of oxygen courses around your body. It's not unusual to feel light-headed after these exercises. For some people, so much oxygen is strange to them, it takes a few moments to adjust. By breathing deeply and regularly in this fashion, you'll find that you'll have more energy and vibrancy in the voice.

https://player.vimeo.com/video/155314034

The importance of oxygen for living and speaking. An average brain weighs about 1.4kg. I weigh 88kg. My brain uses 20% of my body's oxygen which is massively disproportional. Oxygen is the fuel for life and the fuel for the voice. People tend to ignore the importance of their breathing in daily life, after all it's something that just happens. That's true. But when you harness the power of your body's oxygen, you'll see that it's the fuel for thinking as well all other body processes. Ignore it at your peril. If oxygen levels fell from 20% to 17%, that would be the end of life on this planet. Make sure you're getting your share, today.

 https://player.vimeo.com/video/157040272

The speaker's mantra – pause, breathe, change eye contact. Breathing is everything in speaking. If you don't have the fuel for the journey, it's going to be an uncomfortable experience. Make a statement. Pause, breathe, change eye contact. Make another statement. Pause, breathe, change eye contact. Make statements of variable length. Change the pitch and pace of your voice. Pause, breathe, change eye contact. Extending the pause demonstrates greater control. The audience perceive a greater value in the message. That all sounds quite complex, but essentially, we're talking about having a conversation with the audience. We're having conversations all day, every day. Just mix it up.

https://player.vimeo.com/video/155314266

Opening up the airways – breathe, squeeze and release. Sometimes we can feel tense in the upper body. It can be due to travel or too much time at the computer. Whenever I feel uncomfortable in my body, I'll do an exercise like this to shift the oxygens level in my body and release tension in the upper body muscle groups.

 https://player.vimeo.com/video/155748435

Control exercises – ssshhhhhh and ffffffffffff – a consistent sound wave – in public speaking our job is to control the things that we want to control. Top priority is your breath. It's your breath that creates the energy for your words. What gives a great singer control is the ability to hit a good note and maintain that wave. This is why I am no longer allowed at karaoke. Hitting the note and maintaining it consistently is the objective. This simple exercise will help you find that consistency, with practice.

 https://player.vimeo.com/video/155816418

1 - 2 breathing – in this exercise we breathe in for 4 seconds, hold and breathe out for 8. So long as it's done in a controlled fashion, you'll be taking in a good shot of fresh oxygen and dispelling most of it through the exhalation. This pattern of breathing is useful for rigorously exercising the respiratory system.

https://player.vimeo.com/video/155748441

Square breathing - relaxed breathing before you go on stage. This is one of my favourite exercises because it creates a rhythm in the breath. The counting helps you to focus on the numbers and so distracts you from your speech. Breathing rhythmically and smoothly is the best thing to control your heart rate. Once your physiology is under control, your chance of performing to a higher level is greatly enhanced.

 https://player.vimeo.com/video/155820727

The sssssshhhhh sound - developing vocal energy on ssssshhhhh. Take a deep breath and explore the sound ssssshhhhh. Talk it high, talk it low, say it with volume, say it in a whisper. See how many times you can say ssssshhhhh on that same breath. Be prepared to feel a little light-headed having expended a great deal of energy.

 https://player.vimeo.com/video/156476872

Tongue twisters for verbal and vocal dexterity. Tongue twisters are particularly useful for non-native English speakers. For example, in Spanish there is no natural W sound. So, when a Spaniard says the word 'wood', he or she struggles to produce the 'w' sound because they are inexperienced in producing that sound. We call it muscle memory. Tongue twisters that require the sound multiple times are really useful (and for fun the sentences don't need to make sense). Wesley went west working in Weighbridge on the world wide web one Wednesday.

 https://player.vimeo.com/video/156477996

Counting on a whisper – this is a good exercise to test the volume of your breath. Take a deep breath in and count out loud on a whisper. In the video, I manage to get to thirty, but my tummy at that point was really straining. If you reach twenty the first-time round, excellent. As you practice it more, you'll be able to extend your original number and in so doing, demonstrate a greater control over the volume of your breath.

 https://player.vimeo.com/video/157039634

Exploring the Ahhh sound – volume and resonance. Again, we're looking to build consistency in the sound wave. In so doing, the sound will be pleasing and have volume. These exercises are great fun and when you hit a bad note, you should laugh rather than anything else. This is a great opportunity to test and stretch the voice and see and feel your potential for speaking.

 https://player.vimeo.com/video/157039960

Exploring the Ahhh sound for variation – the average person has a range of about three octaves. That's twenty-four discernible notes. Top class professional singers can have five octaves. The problem is that most of us have never really explored our voice so we don't know what it's capable of. By using your voice as a siren, you're able to see which end of the spectrum needs development. Wherever your voice breaks, that's an area to smooth out.

 https://player.vimeo.com/video/157040720

The two fingers exercise is a metaphor to help remember to open the mouth and lips wider to improve the articulation of the words. It also slows down the delivery and reduces ums and ahhs. Do the jaw exercises before you try these and notice how different your mouth feels during as you extend your mouth and lips.

 https://player.vimeo.com/video/157041303

The Ahhhh sound is a vowel sound. The purpose of the exercise is to build volume, resonance and consistency. As you can see, I am still a work in progress. But it's good, even at my age, to surprise yourself with how far you have come.

 https://player.vimeo.com/video/157041626

Vowels and consonants are the building blocks of words. The word 'striking' has eight letters and six consonants and each consonant must be sounded to pronounce the word well. It's a striking example, don't you think?

https://player.vimeo.com/video/157655538

The seven-note descending scale is a wonderful way to develop the voice. So, you should be starting with about three octaves, even if you may not know where they are. You voice will probably be cracking at points which is fine and understandable if you're new to the experience. Start with a note that's comfortable and flow down. As always, we're looking to smooth out the voice at the place where it cracks by working on the consistency of the note.

 https://player.vimeo.com/video/157656683

Exploring the voice through words. Start off with some words that are easy to pronounce. Look up and say them high and soft, look down and say them low and hard. Start with petroleum. Then synthesis. Then try Hyde Park, Green Park. Then choose a small sentence like, I've got a lot of chocolate melting in my pocket. Change the rhythm and intensity of the words. There's no right or wrong way, just keep exploring and building your waves of sound.

 https://player.vimeo.com/video/157763227

The seven-note ascending scale – humming and singing. When we hum, your three head resonators vibrate (throat, mouth, nasal cavity). Put your fingers on your throat and then your nose. Squeeze the fingers on your nose and you'll feel the change in your voice. Your voice is a vibration. By working with these vibrations and exploring them, you'll be developing your voice while having a lot of fun.

 https://player.vimeo.com/video/157764831

Exploring the MAH sound – I probably wouldn't do this one at home in the evening because of the neighbours. This one is 100% fun and it's 100% gold for your vocal development. Depth, resonance and intensity of the voice wave – that's what we're exploring.

 https://player.vimeo.com/video/157770158

AH-OO AH-OO – We're working on double vowel soundings. High, low, up, down, change the intensity, change the volume, change the rhythm. Try OO-AH OO-AH. Yes, monkey noises. If you ever come on one of my courses, I'll tell you a story about when I had summer job in a zoo, long before I became aware of this exercise.

 https://player.vimeo.com/video/157770766

The p, d, g exercise is about rhythm, volume, and intensity while having fun. See how many different ways there are of delivering p, d, g in an interesting way.

https://player.vimeo.com/video/157776037

Humming exercises are particularly useful in demonstrating the voice as a wave of sound, feeling the energy within the body, and illustrating the extensive range between the high notes and the low notes of your voice. Exploring this variation is great fun and if it doesn't bring a smile to your face…

 https://player.vimeo.com/video/157777262

Fun with MAH. Here we're just playing with a sound, activating the energy and seeing what happens. There are no personal breakthroughs without exploration.

 https://player.vimeo.com/video/157778252

Get some tingle in your face by humming. You will have heard Australian aborigines making this strange oscillating humming sound. Keep your mouth closed and move your tongue a little to change the vibration. Explore the depth and intensity of the exercise and after a few minutes you should feel a tingling sensation in your lips and sinus areas. That's a good sign that the exercise is working. This exercise uses a lot of your energy. You may feel light-headed by the end of it.

 https://player.vimeo.com/video/157820429

Vowel and consonant sounds – there's an articulation sheet at the bottom of the document which will provide the backbone of the exercise. As always, we're looking for fluency, rhythm and energy. A smile goes a long way with all exercises.

 https://player.vimeo.com/video/157820676

Plosives – tetetetetah – bebebebah – pepepepah! These are called plosives because they explode off the tongue. The mouth, jaw and lips are working particularly hard in this exercise, plus lots of energy from you. Without the background energy you're not likely to make progress.

 https://player.vimeo.com/video/157929811

The lip trill is another of my favourite and slightly bizarre exercises. Put your lips together and blow. How does that feel, a bit unusual? This time see if you can put a low or a high note on the blow. Practice that for a minute and see if you can get a tingle in your nose and your lips. Try to siren now, low through to high and back. Practice for at least a minute. When you finish laughing, give it another minute.

 https://player.vimeo.com/video/157931504

The 13 note complex scale – possibly my greatest challenge as I can never hit the high note. However, that doesn't mean it will be your greatest challenge. We all have different vocal apparatus. It wouldn't be fair to compare Pavarotti to Shirley Bassey as to who was best at this. Pavarotti practiced for 4-5 hours a day and he was the master... We all need to aim to be the best that we can be. Never compare yourself to anybody else.

 https://player.vimeo.com/video/157932525

Macaroni & Ravioli - food for vocal development. This is a rather silly but joyous exercise. It makes me smile, raises my spirits and does wonders for the voice. Say and sing these words repeatedly with a smile. Put volume and intensity into your voice. Mix it up and enjoy the moment.

 https://player.vimeo.com/video/157933260

Singing vowel soundings - a, e, i, o, u. Another exercise to build a consistent wave of sound. The more you practice your voice, the richer the depth and tone. The more you might surprise yourself with the results.

 https://player.vimeo.com/video/157933864

Vibrato - playing with the intensity and oscillation of the voice. I like this exercise because when I hit a good note and play with it, it gives me a real sense of achievement. As I've said, I am not a singer, but working on the volume and intensity is great fun. I really recommend this exercise as it brings a smile to my face.

https://player.vimeo.com/video/157934796

Vowel transitions are a fun way of finding one sound, A for example and transitioning it to another, E for example. As always, we're trying to build a consistent wave of sound, so avoid pushing the note. Stay relaxed and just see what comes out. With a little practice and determination, you'll find a significant improvement in no time.

INTRODUCTION TO THE DIAPHRAGM AND THE FOUR RESONATORS

Diaphragmatic breathing has two key benefits to the speaker. The first is that quality breath control produces a sustained and energised voice. Oxygen flows through the bloodstream helping to reduce tension in the upper body muscle groups. Secondly, deep breathing floods the brain with oxygen, creates a sense of calm, slows things down and enables you to make better decisions in the moment.

AN EXPLANATION OF THE VALUE OF DIAPHRAGMATIC BREATHING

Upper body warm-up exercises

These exercises are to free up any tension in the head, neck, shoulders, rib cage and the back.

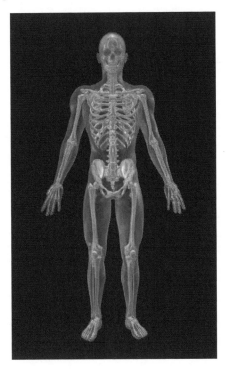

Correct speaking posture

Most importantly, the entire body must be relaxed if the speaker is to score a creditable performance. Muscle tension is the enemy of the speaker.

Correct speaking posture is easily achieved by positioning the soles of the feet shoulder width apart. The knees should be relaxed and flexed. The speaker's torso should be directly supported by the pelvis so that the weight of the upper body is evenly distributed.

When you achieve this balance, your physiology is working to your advantage and most importantly your voice production will flow naturally. For example, if you stand with your feet together, it produces tension in the back of the legs and buttocks. That negative energy is working against you. Some speeches are short and perhaps most people wouldn't notice. But if you're speaking for any length of time (as most speaker/trainers do), you would begin to feel uncomfortable sooner rather than later. Your posture is the foundation upon which your speech is built.

Many people spend endless hours slumped over a computer screen or driving long-distance in their cars. This induces poor posture which creates tension in the upper body where the breathing and speaking apparatus is housed. We need a strategy to remove the tension.

1) starting with the rib cage, set your feet shoulder length apart and gently sway your arms around in front of your body and then behind it. This is a light swaying motion so do not become like a coiled spring. Do this for about thirty seconds. Then gather a little momentum in the swing and raise the arms to chest level. Without straining, aim for a twist of about 270 degrees. You should be feeling warm soon.

Shoulder and jaw loosening exercises

2) now the shoulders – scrunch your shoulders up to the neck for five seconds and then release. Repeat this three times. This exercise works in all muscle groups where we deliberately add tension and then consciously release it. Try it by making a tight fist and then extend the induced tension to the forearms and biceps. After five

seconds of intense tension, release the tension.

3) relieving tension in the jaw is quite easy. Imagine you're chewing gum excessively. You might want to cover your mouth with your hand in public. Now really exaggerate that chewing movement.

4) shoulder rolls: Stand straight and bring the shoulders forwards six times. See if you can touch your ears with your shoulders as they rise. Then bring the shoulders back six times. Then roll and alternate the shoulders forwards and then backwards.

Neck exercise – 180 degrees

5) for the neck - start by looking directly ahead. Then without straining the neck, turn 90 degrees to the right. Extend your arms so that you are looking out directly over your right thumb. Slowly return to the original position and turn left 90 degrees to look out over your left thumb. Slowly repeat this exercise five times. The movement of the neck will help to reduce tension. Lower your arms. Next, from the original starting position, tip the neck backwards, again without straining it too far and hold for five seconds. Then bring the neck all the way down so that it comes as comfortably as possible to touch the upper chest. Repeat three times.

Breathing and bending exercise

6) take a deep breath in and slowly bend down. As your hands come down close to your toes slowly waggle your fingers and then lightly sway your arms. This will relieve any tension in the tummy area. Take a deep breath and then slowly come up one centimetre at a time. Imagine that your vertebrae are stacking up, one on top of the other. As you come up, keep your shoulders and head forwards and down until you stand up straight. Repeat this exercise three times as slowly

as possible. You should feel incredibly relaxed after this.

Stretching and lateral exercises followed by the pantomime yawn

7) an alternative is the pantomime yawn. With arms outstretched wide, take a deep breath, step forward making a horrible extended yawning sound with the mouth as wide open as possible. Repeat three times. This can be quite exhausting.

Vocal warm-up exercises – a quick review

When warming the voice, always work within your physical limitations. If you push yourself too far, there's a danger that you could strain your voice.

a) move the neck and head from left to right as far as you can (i.e. until it starts to feel a strain to move it any further), then relax. Do the same thing forwards and backwards and repeat three times.

b) rotate the head in an anticlockwise circular motion three times. Repeat now clockwise three times.

c) tense the shoulders upwards towards the neck as far as they will go, then relax them with a sudden release of energy. Repeat five times.

d) move the head downwards until the chin presses against the lower neck. Relax, and then move the head backwards as far as you can. Relax again before repeating the routine a few times.

e) chew gum, or tense and relax the jaw a few times.

f) exaggerated yawning to loosen the jaw.

g) put right hand straight up and above the head and move it over to the left. Feel a stretch in the right side about chest height. Repeat on the left hand (3 times each side).

Control exercises

Quality speaking can only be achieved by controlling the breathing apparatus. With concerted practice, control can be achieved quite quickly. In the exercise below, we explore the shh sound, which is not as easy as it sounds. Forming the sound correctly and consistently is all important. Think of the voice as that wave of sound which should be well formed, rounded and with the speaker able to modulate the frequency and intensity at will.

Working on a consistent ssshhhhh sound exercise2

Shhhh! exercise

Breathe in – exhale 1 (second) on 'shh'

Breathe in – exhale 1, 2 on 'shh'

Breathe in – exhale 1, 2 and 3 on 'shh'

Breathe in – exhale 1 – 15 + on 'shh'

'shh' can be substituted for 's' and 'f'

Whispering on a breath

Whisper count - then chant, then speak.

Breathe in, on the exhaled breath try to introduce a sound using the open vowel sound of 'Ah'. Think dentist.

Building a consistent volume with the Ahhh sound

Using the Ahhhh sound as a siren

Discussion on topping up the diaphragm for maximum resonance

Try to coordinate the breathing muscles and the vocal cords so that the attack of the note is neither forced nor breathy.

Now sustain the sound 'Ah' and make it louder and softer, louder and softer.

Speaking slowly with mouth open two fingers wide

When you widen the mouth and speak, you change the entire vocal dynamic. The position and shape of the mouth's cavity is now changed and more air escapes from it. Try talking with your mouth open wider; the impact will be a) to slow down the rate of delivery and b) possibly make your voice sound more refined. This exercise is effective almost immediately and it is one used often in helping people change their sound (especially when they do not like the sound of their own voice).

Breathe in and raise the arms at the sides to shoulder level.

Bend the arms at the elbow and rest the fingers on the nape of the neck.

With the arms in this position and the shoulders well down, breathe in and out.

Exercise to maintain vocal energy on one breath

Now try building up a long sentence, i.e. "I went to the shops and I bought a pen, a book, a pair of socks, a fountain pen (all in one breath). Stop and breathe. Now start again and keep adding items to the list. The objective of this exercise is to maintain vocal quality throughout one consistent breath. Your lungs are enormous. Use them to their maximum.

The resonator scale (open mouth two fingers wide) - Concentrating on vowels.

Exploring the resonator scale

Oo as in through
Oo as in good
Oh as in tone
Aw as in all
O   as in not
Ah as in part
U   as in must
ER as in serve
A   as in and
E   as in then
AY as in shape
I   as in its
EE as in speech

Tone Exercises

Lip vowel, (whispered)

Hah, Hoo, Hah, Hoo, Hah, Hoo, Hah, Hoo, Hah, Hoo.

Tongue vowel, (whispered)

Hah, Hee, Hah, Hee, Hah, Hee, Hah, Hee, Hah, Hee.

Consonant sounds with vowels

Lip and Tongue vowels, voiced

H-AH

H-OO

H-EE

Vowel soundings and consonants

Practice repeating these sequences (voiced)

HAHOO, HAHOO, HAHOO,

HAHEE, HAH EE, HAH EE,

HOOEE, HOOEE, HOOEE,

HOOAH, HOOAH, HOOAH,

HEEOO, HEEOO, HEEOO,

HEEAH, HEEAH, HEEAH,

Head resonators are the throat, nose and mouth

Exercise 1

When expanding the resonator, it's best to start with the position which is normally the most open, the position of the vowel sound AH.

Open jaw and placing the tongue forward is important as it avoids constriction at the two most usual points for tension; at the jaw and the junction of the mouth and throat.

Keep breathing deeply as this increases the size of the pharynx.

Hold one hand behind the ear and one hand in front of the mouth.

Whisper the vowel.

Exercise 2

Maintaining the jaw in its open position, the lips should be rounded to the size of a pencil to make the OO sound. Take care to minimize jaw movement without creating rigidity or tension.

Alternate these positions:

AH, OO, AH, OO, AH, OO, AH, OO, AH, OO, AH, OO

Exercise 3

Starting from the basic AH position and making sure the tongue tip is against the lower teeth, the body of the tongue should be raised high up in front of the mouth. It is especially important to resist the tendency of the lips to spread.

On breathing out we hear the vowel EE.

By raising the tongue, we have diminished the size of the mouth and noticed that in consequence the pitch has risen.

AH, EE, AH, EE AH, EE, AH, EE, AH, EE, AH, EE

For the following exercises use the resonator scale (whispered and voiced)

Exercise 4

Both OO and EE respectively represent extreme positions of the tongue and the lips. Between OO and AH there are four intermediate points:

Oo as in good   oh as in tone   aw as in all   o as in not

By passing through the series from OO to AH we successfully increase the size of the opening and the effect is to increase the size of the resonator.

Exercise 5

In between AH and EE there are six intermediate sounds;

U as in must, ER as in serves, A as in and, E as in then, AY as in shape, I as in its.

The tongue, in moving forwards and upwards, successively diminishes the size of the mouth as a resonator. (Every time the tongue decreases the size of the mouth, it actually increases the size of the pharynx as the sum total of the two cavities together is constant.)

Throat

If you are concerned about constriction in your throat try the following exercise:

Humming on a comfortable mid-range note.

Introducing sound

Exercise 6

Breath pressure to be firm and prefixed by an 'H', which is to begin at the instant of breathing in and out and to cease before you run out of breath.

H-AH H-OO H-EE

The following pairs of vowels should be sung on a centre note:

HAHOO, HAHOO, HAHOO

HAHEE, HAHEE, HAHEE

HOOEE, HOOEE, HOOEE

Finding your range exercise

Humming middle, low and high and the siren

Hum on a comfortable middle note

Find a higher note

Find a lower note

Siren up and down

Join them seamlessly by sliding between them.

Nasal Resonance

Nasal resonance must never be allowed to predominate but when two main cavities of the neck are fully expanded, nasal resonance may be present in the form of an added richness which helps to create a ringing quality.

Insufficient expansion of the other cavities leads to nasality – an inability to open the jaw and the throat. Use the previous exercises to remedy this.

If you want to create some nasal resonance to give balance to your voice, use the following exercises:

Exercise 8

Exploring the Mah sound – high and low

Form the consonant M. Alternate with AH while cupping hands over the mouth and nose.

MAH MAH MAH MAH MAH MAH MAH MAH MAH MAH MAH

The vibrations for the consonant should be felt strongly on the fingers and in passing AH, a trace should remain.

Exploring the resonator scale exercise

Repeat the following words:

Mummy| Ninny | Niminy | Remember the money

Exercising the soft palette

To correct nasality arising from insufficient activity of the soft palate, it is necessary to recognise the sensation accompanying the high arching of the palate.

Exercise 9

Whistle a sustained low note. If the entrance to the nose is closed, this cannot be done.

Yawn. The palate will rise to close the entrance.

Alternate the sounds NG and AH. Jaw fully open and use a whisper.

Breathe on the NG. Exhale on AH. A faint click will be heard as the soft palate rises and the tongue is lowered.

Repeat the name Ingy several times.

Pull a smiley face and hold for 3 seconds.

Pull an angry face and hold for 3 seconds.

Articulation

Clarity of the voice is all important to a successful discourse. Word beginnings and word endings should be crisp and easily understood. Vowel sounds and consonant sounds must be sounded appropriately for it to be easily digested by the audience. The following exercises work through the articulation sheet demonstrating the correct soundings.

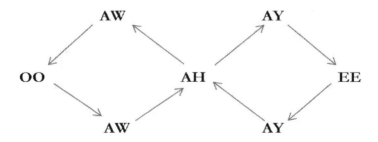

Start with the centre vowel 'AH' and move straight through 'AY' to reach 'EE', and then back through 'AY', through the centre vowel again, to meet 'AW' and then move left to reach 'OO' and then back through 'AW' to end at 'AH'. Repeat x 3.

Example:

HAH HAY HEE - HAY HAH HAW – HOO HAW HAH

Consonant endings

OOK   OHK   AWK   AHK   AYK   EEK
OOKT OHKT AWKT AHKT AYKT EEKT
OOSKT OHSKT AWSKT AHSKT AYSKT EESKT
OOP   OHP   AWP   AHP   AYP   EEP
OOPT OHPT AWPT AHPT AYPT EEPT
OOSPT OHSPT AWSPT AHSPT AYSPT EESPT
OOS   OHS   AWS   AHS   AYS   EES
OOST OHST AWST AHST AYST EEST
OOSTS OHSTS AWSTS AHSTS AYSTS PEESTS

Articulation – Pace – Projection

Use the articulation sheet.

On the sheet you'll see vowels which represent the most open position of the resonator and the most extreme positions of the tongue and lips; EE, AH, OO. To connect these vowels AY and AW are used.

Each vowel, starting with AH is to be prefixed by an 'H'.

HAH HAY HEE – HAY HAH HAW – HOO HAW HAH

Then introduce 'N'. The lips must meet lightly, not tensed together and the tongue must be forward with light vibrations on the lips.

MAH MAY MEE - MAY MAH MAW - MOO MAW MAH

NAH NAY NEE - NAY NAH NAW - NOO NAW NAH

LAH LAY LEE - LAY LAH LAW - LOO LAW LAH

Combining consonant sounds

Then try combining the consonants as rapidly as possible as follows:

MAH NAH LAH MAY NAY LAY
MEE NEE LEE MAY NAY LAY
MAH NAH LAH   MAW NAW LAW
MOO NOO LOO   MAW NAW LAW
Then try TH, V and Z.
MAHNAHLAH   THAVAHZAH
MAYNAYLAY   THAYVAYZAY
MEENEELEE   THEEVEEZEE
MAWNAWLAW THAWVAWZAW
MEENOOLOO THOOVOOZOO

Plosives

Exercises for T and D
Tongue tip against ridge behind upper teeth
Back of tongue free and throat open and relaxed
Flick the tongue against the palate
Tetetete tah
Dedede dah
P and B
Lips engaged but not tense
Pepepepe pah
Bebebebe bah
Memememe mah

Correcting Lazy Ls

Tongue tip against ridge behind teeth

Back of tongue free and throat opened and relaxed

Tip coming to rest behind bottom teeth

Lalalalalalalala

Then use sounds AH to EE on the resonator scale, prefixing them with L.

LAH   LU LER   LA LE LAY   LI LEE

R

Resisting the temptation for the lower lip to meet the upper lip in 'R'. Use your tongue instead. Place your finger on the lower lip while speaking the following sentence.

A serenaded secretary sang sweetly in September.

Be careful when using an 'r' to link the end of one word with another that starts with a vowel. Otherwise 'her ear' can sound like 'her rear'. It's always important to stress the vowel on the following word.

S

A strong S can be pronounced by getting the tongue into the position for T and pronouncing extremely slowly so that the tongue hardly leaves the upper gums, and then directing the breath over it.

Practice:

EE S
AY S
AH S
AW S
OH S
OO S

Attack

Practice saying the sequences as rapidly as possible. Take care to hit all the final consonants to exercise the tongue.

Verbal dexterity exercise

The tense tips of the teeth tremble terribly.

I'm yelling a yodel yonder.

Cranberries and currants are current and creatively credible.

Simon Sadler sadly sat saluting the Saturns.

Projection

Using a throwing action, speak your sentence and try to coordinate movement and sound.

Decide on a short phrase. Speak it at a conversational level. Then step backwards. Speak it again, judging the volume required to reach your imagined listener. Step backwards again, increasing the distance and increasing the volume, without shouting.

Vocal energy

Put your notes by the wall. Then push against the wall while reciting your notes. It will help to deliver a more energetic voice.

p, d, g tongue workout

Say p, d, g pronounced as non-capital letters quickly 10 times. These sounds provide a vocal workout moving the tongue quickly to produce rounded sounds.

M as in pneumatic drill exercise

Bend the knees and extend clasped hands in front of you. Take a deep breath and sound M like a pneumatic drill for the extent of that breath. Repeat three times.

Don't fiddle with the middle bundle of candles

Read only the vowel sounds found in the sentence above – o i e i e i e u e o a e pronounced as non-capital letters. Try this with different sentences for variety.

Read text passages with silly high and low intonation. Learning to play with the voice gives us the opportunity to break out of and explore our normal speech patterns.

Lie flat on your back and put a thick book (3 inches) under the back of your head. Try the earlier breathing exercises with your knees up (semi-supine) and read out a passage of text while lying down.

Singing exercises to warm-up the voice

Humming – 7 note ascending scale

Singing – 7 note ascending – 2 seconds per note with a flourish on the last note.

Humming – 7 note ascending – 5 seconds per note with a crescendo on the last note.

Singing – 7 note descending scale exercise

Humming – 7 note descending – 3 seconds per note with a crescendo on the last note.

Lip trill exercises

Lip trills – basic, then vary higher and lower.

Same again, this time with fingers pressed against cheeks.

Lip trills while swinging the arms.

Complex scale 13 note scale exercise

Vowel singing a, e, i, o, u mah, meh, mih, moh, moo

Ma, me, mi, mo, moooo - flourish on the mooo

laaahgaah laaahgaah laaahgaah x 3 – get that jaw working wide…

Sustain three notes

Ravioli/Macaroni

Vowel transitions e-u, e-o, e-a, e-r, e-or crescendo on last vowel

Sight Reading and Verse Reading

Have you ever read a children's book in a flat and dull voice? Don't be surprised if the child for whom you are reading covers their head with a blanket and pretends to be asleep. A marvellous way of developing the voice is to read children's stories like *Goldilocks* and *Cinderella* and fill the voice with warmth, charm, light and shade. Read it with intonation and expression; bring the subject matter alive in the mind's eye of your audience. This is not easy at first, but with practice a more successful outcome is just around the corner. The immediate benefit will be the recognition that we always need to work the voice for the audience and for ourselves, so that our message is received in the same way that we send it. It is not what we say, but the way that we say it, and in addition, it's how you make people feel. The same is true of verse reading. Interpretation is the key factor that brings delight to the audience.

'The Owl and the Pussy Cat' – Edward Lear

The Owl and the Pussy-cat went to sea In a beautiful pea green boat,

They took some honey, and plenty of money, wrapped up in a five pound note.

The Owl looked up to the stars above, and sang to a small guitar,

'O lovely Pussy! O Pussy my love, what a beautiful Pussy you are,

You are! What a beautiful Pussy you are!'

Pussy said to the Owl, 'You elegant fowl! How charmingly sweet you sing!

O let us be married! too long we have tarried: But what shall we do for a ring?'

They sailed away, for a year and a day,

To the land where the Bong-tree grows

And there in a wood a Piggy-wig stood, with a ring at the end of his nose,

His nose, with a ring at the end of his nose.

'Dear pig, are you willing to sell for one shilling

Your ring?' Said the Piggy, 'I will.'

So they took it away, and were married next day, By the Turkey who lives on the hill. They dined on mince, and slices of quince,

Which they ate with a runcible spoon;

And hand in hand, on the edge of the sand,

They danced by the light of the moon,
The moon, they danced by the light of the moon.

'Sonnet 18' – William Shakespeare

Shall I compare thee to a summer's day?
Thou art more lovely and more temperate:
Rough winds do shake the darling buds of May,
And summer's lease hath all too short a date
Sometime too hot the eye of heaven shines,
And often is his gold complexion dimmed,
And every fair from fair sometime declines,
By chance or natures changing course untrimmed:
But thy eternal summer shall not fade,
Nor lose possession of that fair thou owest,
Nor shall death brag thou wandrest in his shade,
When in eternal lines to time thou growest,
So long as men can breathe and eyes can see
So long lives this, and this gives life to thee.

Tongue twisters to build verbal dexterity

Tongue twisters are a popular method of building verbal dexterity and bringing delight to both the speaker and the audience. The tongue is a muscle, just like all of the other muscle categories in your body and must be worked regularly to ensure top performance. In clear speech, the tongue must be placed in the correct position to produce the correct sound. It is called 'muscle memory'. Imagine the first words that you ever uttered, 'mummy' or 'daddy' perhaps. Do you ever have concerns that you'll be able to produce those sounds? I hope not. Your tongue has produced those sounds thousands of times in your life, and it is muscle memory that does the work.

However, if you are speaking in a second language, it can be difficult to produce the correct sound, especially if the sound does not naturally occur in your native langue.

For example, some students from Nigeria have problems with the 'the' sound. It does not naturally occur in their language so there is no muscle memory to fall back on. This new sound has to be correctly practiced and rehearsed. Practice is the key. Below are some tongue twisters that can be practiced anytime, anywhere, as a group or in private.

Tongue twisters

Raise the retail price. Cricket critic – (say it fast x 3).
A library littered literally with literature.
The rusty rod was wrapped in a rotting rag.
Nine nimble noblemen nibbled nettles.
Seven Severn salmon swallowing shrimps.
Rich Rajas ride reindeers with red rope reins round their regal necks.
Three fluffy feathers fell from feeble Phoebe's fan.
Virile Victor vanquished vain vendors.
Three Scottish thistles in a thicket.
The Archbishop's cat crept craftily into Canterbury Cathedral crypt causing cataclysmic chaos in clerical circles by keeping cunningly concealed.
Old Tommy Taylor, Tailor and retailer.
The crime complete, the coward crept cautiously coastward.
The conundrum constructed by the communist was catastrophic.
Twelve tall tulips turn tilting towards the sun.
He had long legs and leapt easily along the lane.
The rugged ruffian ran raucously around Redhill and Richmond.

Summary

Let's return to the three key messages regarding public speaking:

a) It's not what you say - it's the way that you say it.

b) Know your audience and their expectations. Stay on theme and keep it relevant.

c) Planning, preparation, practice.

Speaking without preparation is like decorating without doing the preparatory work. Papering over the cracks doesn't remove the underlying problem and it is only a question of time before it becomes unsightly. Be professional and prepare well.

And finally, in which aspects of your life are you considered successful? Ask yourself the question, why do you and others believe that you are successful in those fields? Whatever they are, it can be guaranteed that you have spent a great deal of time studying it, practicing it and adjusting it to accommodate all of the inherent variables that can affect a multiplicity of scenarios. That investment in your time and energy has made you an incredibly valuable individual. Your commitment to the task makes you successful.

It's the same with speaking. Commit yourself to the task and you will quickly begin to receive the dividends of becoming an effective and proficient speaker. From that point onwards who knows where your professionalism and speaking skills will take you?

'Our knowledge can only be finite, while our ignorance must necessarily be infinite.' – Karl Popper

I have tried to shoehorn as much valuable information into this book as possible. This is my subjective approach to speaking and it has helped calm the minds of thousands of students over the years. I remain a conscientious student of speaking, science and philosophy. Every book and article I devour takes me one step closer to becoming the speaker that I really want to be. So finally - say the words, feel the words and one day soon you will become the message.

'What we do in life ripples in eternity.' – Marcus Aurelius

I sincerely wish that your endeavours as a speaker bring you the joy and reward that public speaking and training has brought me during a typical lifetime of ups and downs. A life without challenge is a wasted life. It's important that we're constantly stretched to really see where our potential takes us.

There are some aspects of the course that I cannot explain in book form because the class is about the group dynamic. How you relate to other people and how each student is pivotal in the development of their classmates. Everybody is both a speaker and a member of the audience. The fear of public speaking sounds a little scary, but the classes are not. Students leave with smiles and hugs for their colleagues and a sense of accomplishment. They feel good because they've taken action and faced their fears. Now they see their situation through a more positive and realistic lens.

I am busy documenting my work in this book and with the enclosed videos, and there's still more to come. Long after I have gone, I would like my work to touch the lives of others and perhaps allow my daughter's future family an opportunity to get to know me a little through my work and my humour. I may be gone but I'd like my message to continue to ring out from every hillside. 'You can do it! You can do it! Thank God Almighty, you can do it!'

QUOTATIONS

'The real voyage of discovery consists not in seeking new landscapes, but in having new eyes.' – Marcel Proust

'When I let go of what I am, I become what I might be.' – Lao Tzu

'Whenever we proceed from the known into the unknown, we may hope to understand, but we may have to learn at the same time a new meaning of the word 'understanding.' – Werner Heisenberg

'All experience is subjective.' – Gregory Bateson

'Patience is necessary, and one cannot reap immediately where one has sown.' – Søren Kierkegaard

'Ask not what public speaking can do for you, but what you can do for public speaking.' – Anon

'Courage is knowing what not to fear.' – Plato

'The deepest principle in human nature is the craving to be appreciated.' – William James

'A coward dies a thousand deaths, a brave man but once…' – *Julius Caesar* - Shakespeare

'You are all enlightened beings. You are all Buddhas pretending not to be. It is my duty to expose you.' – Bhagwan Shree Rajneesh (Osho)

'It is the mark of an educated mind to be able to entertain a thought without accepting it.' – Aristotle

Heuristics – 'Nothing in life is as important as you think it is when you are thinking about it.' – Daniel Kahneman

'The first principle is that you must not fool yourself and you are the easiest person to fool.' – Richard Feynman

'Never mind the ball – get on with the game.' – Dave McCormack

'The unexamined life is not worth living.' – Socrates

'Fortune favours the prepared mind.' – Louis Pasteur

'Beliefs are overrated.' – Jamie Smart

'Let go of what was. Surrender to what is. Have faith in what will be.'
– Sonia Ricotti

'Every person takes the limits of their own field of vision for the
limits of the world.' – Arthur Schopenhauer

'It is important that you get clear for yourself that your only access to
impacting life is action. The world does not care what you intend,
how committed you are, how you feel or what you think, and
certainly it has no interest in what you want and don't want. Take a
look at life as it is lived and see for yourself that the world only
moves for you when you act.' – Werner Erhard

'The best way to find yourself is in the service of others.' – Mahatma
Gandhi

'All that we are arises from our thoughts.' – The Buddha

'The way you make me feel.' – Michael Jackson

'Nothing changes but everything is different.' – Michael Neill

'The voice inside your head is not the voice of God, although it
sounds like it thinks it is.' – Cheri Huber

'Our deepest fear is not that we are inadequate. Our deepest fear is
that we are powerful beyond measure. It is our light, not our
darkness that most frightens us.' – Marianne Williamson

'You ain't got nothing till you hit rock bottom.' – The Dandy
Warhols

'95% of people experience life through the storm of their thoughts.'
– Mark Twain

'In life you can make your decisions or let other people make those
decisions for you. Being above the influence is about staying true to

yourself and not letting people pressure you into being less than you.' – Anon

'Objectivity is purely subjective.' – Woody Allen

'Reality is an illusion, albeit a persistent one.' – Albert Einstein

'If your joy is derived from what society thinks of you, you're always going to be disappointed.' – Madonna

'Courage is the first of all human qualities because it guarantees all others.' – Winston Churchill

'Try not to become a man of success, but rather try to become a man of value.' – Albert Einstein

'Life is a contact sport.' – Sydney Banks

'The limits of my language are the limits of my world.' – Ludwig Wittgenstein

'You are not who you think you are AND you are so much more.' – Addiction.com

'The way you see people is the way you treat them, and the way you treat them is what they become.' – Johann Wolfgang von Goethe

'The ability to perceive or think differently is more important than the knowledge gained.' – David Bohm

'You are not feeling your circumstances – you're feeling your thinking.' – Michael Neill

'There is nothing either good or bad but thinking makes it so.' – William Shakespeare

'You become what you think about.' – Earl Nightingale

'There is only ever this moment. The present is all there is. The future and past are thought generated illusions. Illusions you only ever experience in the present.' – Jamie Smart

'The secret to success is hard work and intelligent practice.' – Shakira

'The best time to plant a tree was 20 years ago. The second best time is now.' – Chinese Proverb

'We are only ever one thought away from the resolution to any problem.' – William James

'Success is not final and failure is not fatal.' – Winston Churchill

'An expert is a person who has made all the mistakes that can be made in a narrow field.' – Niels Bohr

'Everything happens in a blaze of light.' – WB Yeats

Vulnerability – 'Pressure creates diamonds.' – Dr Ivan Joseph

'Don't be fooled by the simplicity of breathing. It's highly efficient. How could anything so simple be so beneficial? Just remember that the nose is for breathing and the mouth is for eating.' Stig Severinson – World champion freediver.

'The art is concealing the art.' – Sir Lawrence Olivier

'The undiscovered country from whose bourn, no traveller returns.' – William Shakespeare.

'It is impossible to speak in such a way that cannot be misunderstood.' – Karl Popper

'The strength of a man's virtue should not be measured by his special exertions, but by his habitual acts.' – Blaise Pascal

'Our knowledge can only be finite, while our ignorance must necessarily be infinite.' – Karl Popper

'What we do in life ripples in eternity.' – Marcus Aurelius.

TESTIMONIALS

I have over many years witnessed, advised and inspected many teachers and trainers in the UK and worldwide. Vince Stevenson is up there amongst the best. I have seen him transform the spoken communication abilities of, for example, groups of managers, senior police officers, sales personnel and civil society organisers. I have witnessed him instilling self-confidence and the competence to perform well in interviews in school-leavers and disadvantaged youth. I have first-hand evidence of his enabling reticent and nervous individuals to deliver powerful presentations. In terms of exemplary and enjoyable capacity building, Vince is a one-off.

Mike Douse (International Educational Development Advisor (for EU, DfID, UNICEF and other agencies) and author of *An Enjoyment of Education*)

Vince Stevenson is the 'real deal' when it comes to public speaking training. Upon noticing his presence and credentials at an event in Bucharest it immediately propelled me to attend, figuring I could learn a lot. It was the best move I could make. Vince is experienced, inspiring and he has a kind demeanour when it comes to helping someone with their speaking skills. Forget the fluff and empty promises from many training firms – this man has substance and I encourage everyone to listen to him. I'm glad I did!

Paul Renaud (Executive Coach & Author, *A Networking Book*)

I have a distinct recollection of Vince's public speaking workshop with a group of people who stutter in Malta. Vince offered to collaborate with me during a public speaking training course launching the

Stuttering Association of Malta. He presented as a human, caring and passionate professional. His enthusiasm was inspiring. His training changed the way participants look at an audience. The course was dynamic, fun and replete with useful strategies and techniques. Participants claimed that 'I have found it to be a life changing experience' and 'I'm surprised with the progress I made'. The training was a moment of personal satisfaction and fulfilment for both of us. Vince is certainly an 'excellent confidence booster'.

Dr. Joseph Agius - University of Malta

I met Vince some years ago when he was the Chairman of my local speakers' club in London. Under his direction, myself and the club members developed our confidence and speaking skills in double quick time. His training has helped me enormously in my career where I regularly facilitate meetings for up to 40 people and I use his objective, supportive and constructive feedback framework almost every day. In recent years, Vince has run a number of projects at my consultancy and he's one of our most popular coaches.

Anandha Ponnampalam – Sapient Global Markets

Vince is the embodiment of the art and craft of public speaking. His years of experience is blended with authentic and stylish delivery. He is a joy to listen to and learn from. While most trainers draw inspiration from the books and speeches of others, he speaks honestly and humorously from the highs and lows of his professional experience. Once you finish reading the book, make sure to join one of his courses if you have not done so already. It might be one of the best investments you ever make.

Alex Glod – The Art of Storytelling – Bucharest

I have nothing but praise and admiration for the work of Vince Stevenson. During a period when my public speaking efforts needed bolstering in content, approach and impact, we began our work together across continents via the wonders of Skype. His approach is confidence boosting, unique, and powerful. He was able to inject gravitas, structure and purpose to many of my presentations and helped me to find my voice, message and performance. He is professional, discreet and focussed. His efficiency, gentle warmth and genuine support are second to none. His book is an important addition to your bookshelf...

Jennifer Francis (Pennsylvania)

ABOUT THE AUTHOR

Vince Stevenson (The Fear Doctor) - Speaker - Trainer - Author

Continuing Practice

If you live in and around London, Vince runs a monthly Executive practice session from 7pm to 9pm. Former students who wish to practice elements of their speech and its delivery are welcome to come along. Please contact me directly for details.

Vince is a speaker/trainer who has won a number of awards for leadership, education and development. He is a founder of the College of Public Speaking London and works as Education Director managing all aspects of course delivery and content. He is also one of the UK's leading speech coaches and has worked with leaders across the spectrum of politics, industry, finance as well as featuring largely in a humanitarian role.

Vince is an avid learner and in recent years has accomplished a number of certificates in Learning and Communication Science with the University of California, San Diego, the University of Amsterdam, and Instructional Design with the Institute of Adult Learning, Singapore.

Vince is a qualified teacher/trainer and over the last fifteen years his enthusiastic membership of several voluntary organisations has helped to raise the awareness and standards of effective communication. He is the trusted adviser behind the College's outstanding 'pro bono' service to the Third Sector.

In recent years Vince has delivered sessions for the Civil Service in Mauritius, various programs at Insead International Business School near Paris, and at the Asia Foundation, Save the Children and BRAC in Bangladesh. He has assisted the development of the TEDx Storytelling project in Bucharest. He has also been guest speaker at LSE, UCL, KCL and SOAS as well as the University of Malta. He is a regular contributor at St Mungo's Recovery College, London. From 2016-18 Vince featured in a two-week education and cultural exchange at the Zajel Youth Exchange Program, An-Najah University in Palestine, an experience he describes at the highlight of long and rewarding career in education.

Vince is also a specialist in vocal development techniques and runs regular workshops. He loves helping people overcome their fear of public speaking and is facilitator for the College of Public Speaking's ground breaking Fear of Public Speaking Retreat. He also coaches groups and individuals in achieving excellent interview results.

Before founding the College of Public Speaking London in 2006, Vince was an IT analyst working mostly in the financial and energy sectors. Vince became a freelance trainer with Sun Microsystems and then with Oracle.

Printed in Great Britain
by Amazon

84253493R00147